THE ROSE QUESTION-AND-ANSWER BOOK

THE ROSE
QUESTION-AND-ANSWER
BOOK

by John Milton

HEARTHSIDE PRESS INCORPORATED

Publishers • New York

Drawings by Eva Melady except for those on pages
12, 13 and 105, which are by Richard Houseal

TABLE OF CONTENTS

FOREWORD

I have been growing roses for a number of years. What has impressed me most about them is their ability to give me satisfactions that far outweigh the care I have given them. I have also been writing about roses for a number of of years, and, with particular reference to a part of that work having to do with original descriptions of new rose inventions, I have had some notable adventures. For me, at least, it is an adventure to stand before a new rose for the first time: to study it, to try to evaluate it objectively, and then to interpret and translate its personality into the written word to be read by some unknown gardener far away. I fear that more than once I have not been able to tame my own enthusiasm; I hope that any lapse in my objectivity has not led that far off gardener astray . . . his eyes, on seeing the same rose in his garden, perhaps not telling him what mine had told me.

But then a curious thing happens. The gardener writes to me, complaining strongly, if not bitterly, that I have failed to do justice to the rose, which has become his pet. I have under-rated it. I have not caught its true quality nor been swayed enough by its rare beauty. Then, as though to mollify what he thinks might be my ruffled feelings, he grudgingly admits that I was right about the bloom being six inches wide. (What he does not know, and which I admit here, is that I am pleased by his disagreement.) He goes further and asks a question or two, thus admitting his own ignorance and setting me up again on my pedestal as an authority, and as his superior. On the other hand, perhaps it is I who is being led astray by this irate gardener!

I am nonetheless glad to have his letter and to be able to answer his questions; for among people who love roses it is always a pleasure to help if one can.

The purpose of this book is to provide help and information in a handy package; the basis for its question-and-answer form lies in the accumulation over the years of kinds of questions in various categories which have come to me and my associates in letters or in face-to-face encounters with rose gardeners. The book does not pretend to be an encyclopaedia, concise or otherwise. It does not carry every last scrap of information ever garnered on the general subject of roses. It does pretend to basic facts that can help the amateur rose gardener not only in the growing of roses but also in those broader areas affecting a general understanding of roses, and a better appreciation of what goes into their creation.

I am indebted to a number of people: to all those gardeners who have asked questions and have needed help; to Mr. George M. Hart, Rose Consultant and Lecturer of The Conard-Pyle Company, on whose sound judgment and superior knowledge I have drawn many times; and, far from least, to all those other writers about roses whose work has fed my appetite for information over the years.

John Milton

Chadds Ford, Pennsylvania

THE ROSE QUESTION-AND-ANSWER BOOK

I THE KINDS OF ROSES

All over the world, millions of gardeners are growing roses. Rose types (or classes as they are sometimes called) of principal interest to the contemporary gardener are Hybrid Teas, Grandifloras, Floribundas, Climbers, Miniatures, Tree Roses and Shrub Roses. Each type of rose has a typical appearance and growth habit by which it can be identified.

Q. *What is the difference between a rose type or class and a variety?*

A. It's like this: an automobile is a type or class of conveyance or vehicle. A Chevrolet is a named variety of the class called automobile. It's the same with roses. The rose Peace is a named variety of the class called Hybrid Tea.

1. BUSH ROSES

Q. *What is a Hybrid Tea?*

A. The Hybrid Tea rose plant produces large, well-shaped blooms, usually 1 to the stem but sometimes 2 or 3. The solid substance of the flower, the large leaves and the beau-

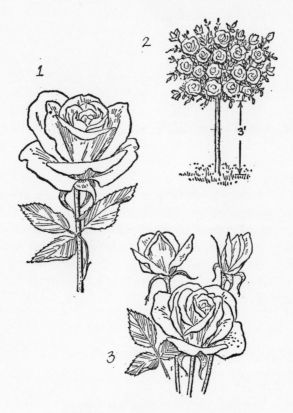

(1) Hybrid Tea; (2) Tree Rose; (3) Grandiflora.

tiful form of bud and bloom are characteristics that make identification easy and explain the popularity of this class of rose. The flowers are often 6 or more inches across when fully open. Gracefully outcurling petals are the rule rather than the exception. The half to fully open flower is generally high-centered, cupped or urn-shaped. The

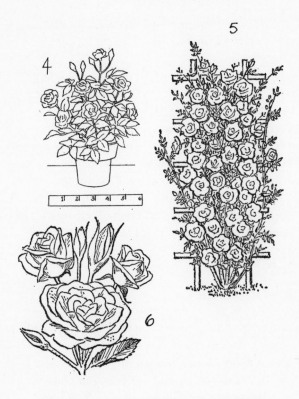

(4) Miniature; (5) Climbing Rose; (6) Floribunda.

plant itself tends to have long stems and strong, thick
canes. It is called "Hybrid" because it is a variety produced by crossing 2 other varieties; and "Tea" because
this class was once thought to have smelled like tea leaves.
Although the name is hardly one with scientific basis, it
has remained with us, inept though it is.

Q. *I understand that a Grandiflora is something like a Hybrid Tea. What are the differences?*

A. The Grandiflora resembles, or has characteristics of, both the Hybrid Tea and the Floribunda. Its flowers tend to have the form of the Hybrid Tea but are generally smaller. On the other hand, this class produces more flowers at one time, and they are likely to come several to the stem rather than singly. Grandifloras are apt to grow taller than Hybrid Teas or Floribundas. There are only a few varieties available to date, but more are being developed each year. The first Grandiflora rose to win an All-America award (in 1955) was Queen Elizabeth.

Q. *What is a Floribunda?*

A. The name means many flowers. The Floribunda produces more flowers at any one time than either the Hybrid Tea or the Grandiflora. Flowers are small, usually from 3 to 4 inches in diameter, and are borne in clusters. Petals are smaller, and fewer as a rule. Form of the open flower is likely to be flattish. Foliage is smaller than that of either the Hybrid Tea or the Grandiflora. With their masses of flowers, Floribundas are very colorful and are most often used in the garden for color effect.

2. CLIMBING ROSES

Q. *What is a Climber? Does it really climb?*

A. A Climber produces long canes that often reach 12 to 15 feet or more. These canes must be supported by a trellis, fence or wall to which it is necessary to tie them in order to maintain some semblance of order and beauty. The Climber is not a climbing plant in the same sense in which ivy or clematis is; that is, it does not fasten itself to its support by clinging tendrils. Nonetheless, in the rose family, this long-caned rose is called a Climber.

Q. *What kinds of Climbers are most popular?*

A. Two kinds of Climbing Roses are in general use today —Repeat Bloomers and Everbloomers. The former, as its name implies, blooms in spring and again in fall; the latter flowers throughout the season. Climbers, unlike Hybrid Teas, Grandifloras and Floribundas which are bush types, do not produce flowers until the second year. However, some of the newer varieties of Everbloomers will have a few flowers in the first season. Climbers are enormously vigorous, growing fast and filling a large area quickly.

Q. *Are flowers on Climbing Roses good for cutting?*

A. Flowers are generally well-formed and very numerous. Many varieties have stems long enough for good cutting.

Q. *What is a Rambler Rose?*

A. A large plant with smallish flowers which blooms profusely once each season. Because it is not remontant (meaning to bloom again) and has an invasive quality, Ramblers are not particularly popular in the small modern garden.

Q. *What is a Trailing Rose?*

A. A Trailing Rose is a Climber suitable for planting on walls or banks, which makes it a useful ground cover.

Q. *What is a Pillar Rose?*

A. A sort of shorter stockier Climber with canes reaching 8 feet or so in length.

3. TREE ROSES

Q. *What is a Tree Rose?*

A. This interesting form of rose results from a special propagative method. It is a small tree with a trunk about 3 feet tall, 1 inch or so in diameter, at the top of which are the branches, foliage and flowers of a rose bush. Tree Roses are like their counterparts except that they have tall trunks. Any variety of rose can be budded or grafted to the taller understock to create a Tree Rose.

Q. *What class of rose can make a Tree Rose?*

A. Roses of any class. Thus there are Hybrid Tea Tree Roses, Floribunda Tree Roses, etc. Some Tree Roses are budded with 2 or 3 different varieties to create 2 or 3 different colors of flower on the same plant.

Q. *What is a Standard Rose?*

A. Same as a Tree Rose.

4. MINIATURE ROSES

Q. *What is a Miniature Rose?*

A. The Miniature Rose is a separate and distinct species of rose with its own permanent characteristics and qualities. It is not, as is sometimes supposed, a dwarfed or stunted rose. Miniatures resemble Hybrid Teas in all respects except in size. Flowers are only as large as a nickel or a quarter, with petals proportionately small. Buds, foliage, stems, branches and thorns are all in keeping with the smallness of the flowers. The plant itself grows usually to a height of from 8 to 12 inches. Jewel-like in all details, the Miniature Rose has great charm, and its appeal lies (as is the case with many small things) in the perfection of its minute parts as they relate to comparable parts of the large, garden roses.

Q. *Is a Miniature Rose very fragile and tender?*

A. No, it is just as rugged, tough and hardy as its larger sisters, and will grow and last in the outdoor garden just as long.

Q. *Can a Miniature Rose be made into a tree?*

A. Yes, the Miniature Rose can be propagated in tree form. It has a trunk about 1 foot tall and ½ inch or so in diameter, at the top of which are the miniature branches, foliage and flowers of its type.

5. OLD-FASHIONED ROSES

Q. *My neighbor always tells me with great pride that he grows only "old-fashioned roses." What exactly are they?*

A. Like hobbyists who dote on antique cars or guns, there is a small group of collectors who plant only roses from an earlier era. These include classes called Alba, Bourbon, China, Centifolia or Cabbale, Damask, Gallica or French, Moss, Noisette, and Tea Rose, with possibly 2 or 3 more. Hybrid Perpetuals, Polyanthas and Ramblers, while comparatively more recent, have also been superseded. These old-fashioned roses may be found in old gardens, but they are no longer cultivated commercially to any extent.

Q. *What is a Shrub Rose?*

A. All roses are either vines (climbers) or shrubs (bushes) since a shrub by definition is any woody-stemmed leafy garden plant. However the term is sometimes used by oldtimers in referring to plants suitable for hedging or as specimens standing alone. Such plants generally are strong growing, with small dense leaves and relatively small flat flowers. Most of the Shrub Roses used today are old varieties. Few new ones are being developed since the demand is not great.

Q. *What is a Bedding Rose?*

A. Again this is a rather old-fashioned term for a group of roses (other than shrubs) used in special garden beds. Most roses available today are Bedding Roses. These include Hybrid Teas, Miniatures, and Floribundas.

II SOIL PREPARATION AND IMPROVEMENT

6. SOIL PROBLEMS

Q. *Do I need special soil to grow roses?*

A. Roses are a rugged breed and will grow in good garden soil with little preparation. Many a successful gardener has done little more than dig a hole for the plant. My own preference however is to prepare the soil as mentioned in section 9.

Q. *Can I plant roses in a clay soil?*

A. Yes, if you treat soil first. To improve soil, work in leaf mold, manure, humus or peat moss before planting— 1 part peat moss to 2 parts soil.

Q. *Can I plant roses in sandy soil?*

A. Yes, if you treat soil first. Work in 1 part of leaf mold, manure, humus or peat moss to 2 parts of soil. Since

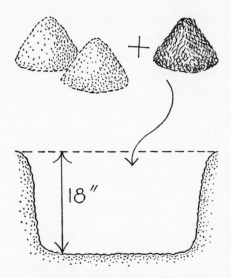

Improve soil with 2 parts soil to 1 part peat moss

water moves fast through sandy soil, the plants may not get the moisture they need so more frequent watering will be necessary.

7. TESTING SOILS

Q. *How can I have the soil tested?*

A. Dig down 8 inches in the area you want to plant roses and take about a pint of soil. Your county agricultural agency or local advertisements will give you names of commercial soil-testing laboratories. Home kits for testing soil are also available but results have to be interpreted, the hardest part of the job.

Q. *I've seen the symbol "pH" used in connection with soils. What does it mean?*

A. "pH" is a symbol in chemistry used to indicate "potential of Hydrogen" in the soil. For example, pH 7. is neutral; pH 6. is on the acid side; pH 8. is on the alkaline side. Roses do best in soils that are neutral or slightly acid. Roses will tolerate a greater degree of acidity than of alkalinity. If soil is too acid, the pH can be raised by adding lime.

Q. *What is considered to be good drainage?*

A. Most soils except very heavy clay kinds are porous enough for water to settle through them. If water collects and remains on the surface for several hours after a rain or if soil is sandy, it should not be planted with roses unless it can be improved. (See section 6.)

8. IMPROVING SOIL

Q. *Can infertile soil be improved so it will grow roses well?*

A. Of course. All you need to do is to add sufficient organic matter and food. Make a mixture of 1 part of organic material (peat moss, rotted manure, humus or compost) and 2 parts of your existing soil. For each 100 square feet of rose bed to be prepared, mix in 4 pounds of balanced fertilizer. The bed should be prepared to a depth of about 18 inches.

Q. *How can I treat soil which is too alkaline?*

A. Acidify the soil by working in 5 to 10 pounds of sulfur for every 100 square feet of soil. Keep adding sulfur every few months for as long as the soil tests alkaline.

Q. *A low spot in my garden gets enough sun for roses. Should I plant there?*

A. Any low spot on a property into which water drains is not a good location for roses. In such poorly drained location, it might be practical to build a raised bed about a foot above ground level, and bring in good soil.

9. PREPARING THE BED

Q. *How do I prepare a rose bed for the actual planting?*

A. Dig up the soil 15 to 18 inches deep. Mix in 1 part peat moss to 3 parts soil. Include ½ a handful or so of fertilizer for each bushel of mixture. Mix well.

Q. *When should I dig up the bed for planting?*

A. Dig up the bed 1 week or 2 in advance if possible. This means that there will be less settling of soil after the planting is done and the plants are more likely to remain at proper level. However to prepare the bed in advance is more of a convenience than a necessity.

Q. *What if I want to plant only 1 rose bush?*

A. Just dig a hole large enough to hold the roots when they are spread out. Two-feet square will be about right. Prepare the soil as in section 8.

10.   PEAT MOSS

Q. *Why use peat moss in the soil?*

A. Peat moss is a fibrous, organic material that is dug from bogs and processed or refined for garden use. When mixed with soil, it lightens it, permits the entry of needed air, helps the drainage and at the same time aids in retaining moisture for the root system. In sandy soils, drainage is too fast and peat moss keeps moisture available. In clay soils, drainage is slower and peat moss by lightening soils creates better flow of water through the soil. Peat moss is invaluable in any planting.

Q. *How much peat moss do you recommend be added to soil?*

A. It is never necessary to use more than equal parts of peat moss and soil. To use more peat moss than soil would make the composition too light for good planting. If soil is hard and claylike, use 1 part peat moss to 1 part soil; if sandy or light in composition, use 1 part peat moss to 2 parts soil; if soil is good average garden soil, use 1 part peat moss to 3 parts soil.

Q. *How often should peat moss be added to soil?*

A. Peat moss should be incorporated in soil only when you are planting or transplanting a rose. It should be placed on the surface of the soil as a mulch whenever it is needed.

11.   FERTILIZER

Q. *If a little fertilizer is good in the soil, why not use a lot?*

A. With roses, too little food is better than too much. An excess of fertilizer will cause stunted growth and small and few flowers.

Q. *Suppose I over-fertilize roses. Can I do anything about it?*

A. Yes. Water plants profusely for the first week to dilute the excessive fertilizer.

III THE FIRST PLANTING

12. WHAT TO DO WHEN THE ROSES ARRIVE

Q. *Must I plant the roses as soon as they arrive from the nursery?*

A. Quick planting is best but if weather is bad, or planting must be delayed for other reasons, leave the package in an unheated garage, cellar or other cool place for a few days until you are ready.

Q. *I have read about heeling-in of roses? Is this necessary?*

A. Yes, if planting will be delayed more than a few days. Take the plants out of the package and set them in a trench in a shaded place in the garden. Cover the roots with soil and spray with water so that soil stays moist. Bury the entire plant if you must delay planting for an extended time. Heeled-in plants which are completely covered with soil will remain in good condition for weeks.

Q. *What's a good way to prevent roses from drying out during the actual planting?*

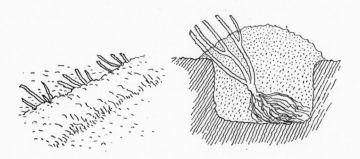

Heel in if planting is delayed

A. Keep roses in their packages. Do not unwrap until you're ready to put the plant in the hole. If you have opened a package containing several plants and there is a delay in planting, plunge roots or opened plants into a bucket of water. You can use the water to soak the soil when the rose is partly planted.

13. HOW TO PLANT ROSES

Q. *What is the best way to plant?*

A. Set the plant in the hole (sections 9 and 17) so that the knuckle, or bud union (where tops and roots join), is at ground level. Many gardeners build a small cone of soil in the hole onto which they set the plant. In this way, they adjust the height of the plant easily. Spread the roots outward so that they will not be cramped, and fill in the hole with prepared soil, making sure that no air pockets remain. When the hole is ¾ full, fill the remaining space with water and allow it to drain through the soil. This will settle the soil firmly around the roots. Fill with water

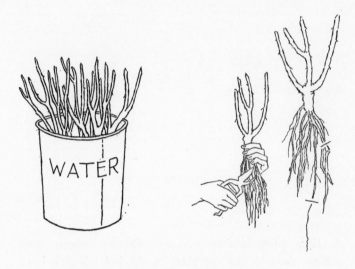

Keep roots moist by soaking new plants in water;
prune off any broken roots.

again, and when this has soaked into the earth add more
soil to ground level. If you had dug the hole and prepared
the soil in advance, you would, of course, first remove the
soil from the hole and then follow the procedure above.

14. BUD KNUCKLE

Q. *Suppose when the rose is planted I find that the
knuckle is slightly above or below ground level. Is this
so critical that I should replant the rose?*

A. Not at all. If the knuckle is an inch or so above or
below ground level, it is perfectly all right. The ground
level rule is merely a guide to the ideal planting. The rose
will grow equally well with the knuckle at ground level
or just above or below it, but some people think the bed

is neater if knuckle does not show. In any case, avoid placing the knuckle more than an inch either way.

15. TAMPING NOT TRAMPING

Q. *Is it necessary when planting to "firm" the soil in the hole or bed by tramping on it or tamping it?*

A. There is no harm in patting the soil gently with your foot, exerting only the slightest pressure. But never tramp on it. Actually, the action of water seeping through the soil is sufficient to settle it. Damage is often done under the misapprehension that the soil should be forced down tightly. When this is done, the soil is so compacted that good growth is hindered. Compaction forces needed air from the soil and causes bad drainage conditions. It also makes watering difficult.

16. DRIED OR BROKEN ROOTS

Q. *A friend of mine always soaks the roots of roses before he plants. Is this good practice and why?*

A. Yes, it's a good idea. The practice insures that the roots go into the ground in moist, pliable condition. Many people immerse the root systems in a bucket of water for an hour or so while preparing to plant, or leave them in water overnight. In cases where the roots may have dried a bit in transit, it is beneficial to soak the entire plant, roots and tops, in water for 12 to 24 hours before planting. This is not to say that if you did not soak the roots the plant would not grow. However, soaking is helpful.

Q. *Suppose plants arrive with broken roots or shoots. Is pruning necessary?*

A. Yes, cut off broken branches or any broken roots with a pruning shears. Most nurseries send out plants which are already top-pruned.

17. BASIC STEPS

Q. *Please summarize the basic steps of making a new rose planting.*

a) Dig up the bed.
b) Mix 1 part peat moss to 2 parts soil; add ½ a handful or so of commercial fertilizer.
c) Make a little hill or cone in the planting hole by mounding up soil.
d) Plant rose bush, spreading out the roots around hill in the direction and shape they grew in. Add soil until hole is ¾ full. Water to top of hole. When water drains off, water again.
e) When water has soaked into earth, fill hole with soil to ground level.
f) Label the plant with name of variety. You can buy many good labels to stake into the ground.
g) In all climates, protect newly planted rose bushes in spring or fall by mounding earth into the canes to a height of 8 to 10 inches. Remove mound when new growth is apparent.

IV WHERE TO PLANT ROSES

Q. *What about planting locations? Is there a right or a wrong place to plant roses?*

A. Roses should never be planted where soil drainage is poor, or where water collects and stands, nor should they be planted in full shade.

18. WIND

Q. *Is a windswept location bad?*

A. A windy site is apt to be dry in summer and cold in winter. Since wind increases evaporation of moisture from roses, avoid a spot that's too exposed. But if you have no choice, better to plant roses in a poor spot than not at all! Give them proper care in preparation, planting and maintenance and you will see them respond gratefully even though the location is not ideal.

Q. *I intend to plant Tree Roses at the entrance to our garden on Long Island which gets a lot of wind at times. Can they survive wind and freezing weather?*

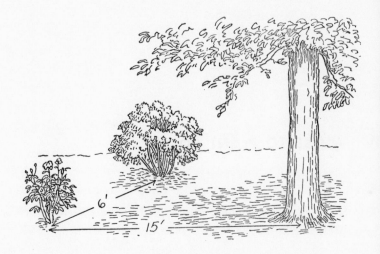

Plant roses 15 feet from shade trees, 6 feet from shrubs

A. Very unlikely. Either 1 or the other can be damaging. However, your best chance lies in the following procedure: lay the roses flat on the ground before freezing weather when the plant is dormant. Cover the top and trunk with soil. You will have to dig up some of the root ball so you can lay the tree on its side without breaking the trunk. In that case cover the root ball too. If the soil is swept away cover with more soil. Cover the soil with evergreen boughs or tar paper held down by rocks.

19. SUN

Q. *How much sun do roses need?*

A. All they can get. They must have at least 5 or 6 hours of sunshine a day—the more the better. If there is a choice of morning or afternoon sun, give them the morning sun.

Q. *My prospective rose garden gets constant sun. Can I be sure my roses won't get too much?*

A. Roses like full sun best—but put 2 or 3 inch mulch of peat moss around the plant to keep moisture and prevent surface from becoming baked. An added bonus—no weeds—will keep the gardener cool too.

20. INTERFERENCE FROM TREES AND SHRUBS

Q. *How far away from trees and shrubs should roses be planted?*

A. Many people make the mistake of planting too closely, failing to consider that as plants grow they take up more room. Keep roses at least 15 feet away from the maximum spread of large trees and evergreens, and 6 feet from large shrubs. When planted too close to roses, the trees and shrubs rob the roses of food, and also are likely to put them too much in the shade.

Q. *The only place for a rose garden is in a sunny corner of my property which unfortunately is overrun with roots from a neighbor's shrubs. What can I do about these roots?*

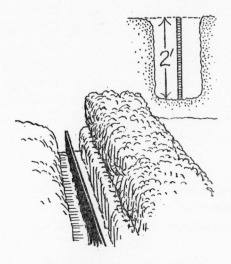

Metal barrier between roses and neighbor

A. Make a barrier between neighboring shrubs and the site of the garden by digging a narrow trench about 2 feet deep. You can put the soil back, but will have to dig up the trench every spring or 2 to keep roots away. A metal barrier 2 feet deep can be set into the trench as a permanent barrier.

21. NEAR HOUSE FOUNDATIONS

Q. *Can roses be planted next to the foundations of a house?*

A. Why not? More and more, landscape designers are using roses for this purpose—but plant properly. Keep 2 or 3 feet away from the foundations to give them room to develop and to provide air circulation. Be sure to dig the area sufficiently deep to uncover stray bits of wood, concrete and other debris left behind by the builder. Test to see whether the soil close to the foundation has become too alkaline through the leaching of cement into it. This can be offset by peat moss. Make a heavier-than-usual application and mix it into the soil. The peat moss will counteract alkalinity.

Q. *My house has overhanging eaves that keep rain from reaching the area underneath. Can I plant roses under the eaves?*

A. Only if you are prepared to water your roses more often and more heavily. Mulch to preserve moisture (section 10).

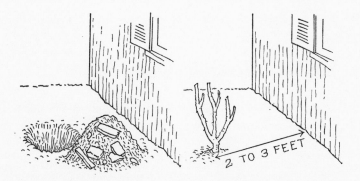

Planting near house, dig deep, remove building debris; not too close

22. HOW FAR APART

Q. *How far apart should roses be from each other?*

A. From 20 to 30 inches is a good rule to follow in spacing your plants. Closer spacing than 20 inches does not give plants enough growing room; more than 30 inches makes them stand too much alone to be part of the rose bed planting plan.

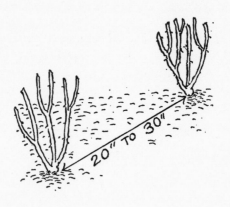

23. FLORIDA

Q. *Can roses be grown anywhere in Florida?*

A. Roses will grow anywhere in the country provided that they are given proper conditions for growth and proper care. In Florida where the growing season is long and sub-tropical conditions force rapid growth, it is difficult for roses to find a period of dormancy that is long enough. Since roses must have rest periods, they are unlikely to live as long in Florida as they do elsewhere, but they are grown successfully in that state by people who give them extra care.

Q. *I retired to Florida and our garden has poor soil. Parts are too sandy; other spots have poor drainage. What to do? I must have at least a few roses.*

A. Since Florida soil is likely to be very porous or very water-logged, many people "import" garden soil from out-of-state. In areas where water remains close to the soil surface (bad drainage), roses can be grown in raised beds. In other places where drainage is too rapid, use plenty of water-retaining peat moss.

24. ALASKA

Q. *How about growing roses in Alaska?*

A. Roses are grown successfully in sheltered valley areas. Though the season is short there, the daylight hours are long and the sun gets hot.

Q. *What special procedure must I follow to grow roses in Alaska?*

A. The wide variations in temperature, the long hours of daylight and the short growing season all pose problems for rose growing in Alaska—but it is being done by enthusiasts. Procedures to follow are: choose varieties known to be especially hardy or carefree (your rose grower's catalogue usually tells this); plant in a sheltered area if possible, or provide shelter; protect in winter by either removing plant bodily from the soil when it is dormant and storing in a cool cellar, or by burying the plant in the garden. Shrub roses in particular are known to do well in Alaska, among them the variety called The Fairy. A new kind named Sea Foam is just as hardy and will doubtless do well too.

V WHEN TO PLANT ROSES

Q. *My neighbor plants roses in fall but I've heard that spring is the better time. Which is correct?*

A. Both are good times if you live in the middle tier of states; spring is right for most of New England and other colder areas; the early winter months are right for the deep south.

25. FALL PLANTING

Q. *Are there any advantages in fall planting?*

A. Yes. The ground is mellow and easily workable in fall. The weather is more predictable. There are fewer demands upon your gardening time. Fall planted roses can take advantage of any break in the weather and temperature to get started sooner, and are thus likely to become established a bit earlier when spring comes. Provided, of course, that climate permits.

Q. *What is the objection to fall planting in the colder states?*

A. Unestablished roses need special protection against severe cold. The commercial nursery is better able to store dormant roses over winter and to send them to you fresh for spring planting. Of course you can plant in the fall even when the weather is not ideal but you will have to take a greater gamble. Once roses are established in Northern gardens and have a good spring and summer growth behind them, they will survive winters with only reasonable protection.

26. SPRING PLANTING

Q. *What is the advantage of spring planting?*

A. There's a big psychological advantage. You know that your roses will soon show growth and will bloom in a few weeks. Spring just seems to be the natural time to plant. Aside from this, there is actually no physical or practical advantage except where weather is severe, since a spring-planted rose does not run the risk of being injured by a winter whose frosts it was not exposed to! In justice to the rose, however, it must be said that a properly planted and protected rose, when planted in fall, almost always comes through safely, especially if it is healthy in the first place.

27. WINTER PROTECTION

Q. *If planted in spring, do roses need protection?*

A. Yes, always build a mound of soil around the bottom of the bush after planting. Remove it only after you have observed that growth has started.

Q. *If planted in fall in moderate climates, do roses need winter protection?*

A. If local winter temperatures do not go below about 15°F., most roses do not need protection. However, if you live where the thermometer drops sharply even occasionally in the winter, play safe and protect the roses with a soil mound.

Q. *Garden writers never specify the exact dates meant by fall and spring. Aren't these general terms subject to interpretation according to the weather?*

A. Yes. Fall is referred to as being from November 1 until frost makes digging impossible; spring, as soon as the ground is workable and danger of frosts is more or less over.

28. PLANTING TIME FOR EVERY SECTION

Q. *When should roses be planted in New England?*

A. Fall or spring in warmer parts; spring in colder parts.

Q. *When should roses be planted in the Middle Atlantic States?*

A. Both fall and spring are good.

Q. *What's the best time to plant in Florida and the Gulf States?*

A. Anytime from November to January 15.

Q. *What's the best time to plant in the Midwest?*

A. Fall or spring, again depending on the incidence of cold.

Q. *What's the best time to plant in the Mountain States?*

A. Plant in spring only.

Q. *When should roses be planted in the Western States?*

A. From December to April 1, depending upon local conditions.

VI TRANSPLANTING

29. DORMANT-SEASON TRANSPLANT

Q. *When is the best time to transplant roses?*

A. After a rose goes dormant in the fall and any time thereafter until spring growth is about to begin, transplanting is safe. During this period roses can be moved about at will without damage to them.

Q. *How should a dormant plant be transplanted?*

A. Simply dig the plant up and replant it where you want it. Take care to dig deep enough to get below the root system so that you will not break the roots. Shake off the soil, put the roots in a bucket of water and move the plant to the new location. Replant it as you would a new rose and hill it up. See chapter III.

30. GROWING-SEASON TRANSPLANT

Q. *Can roses be transplanted at any other time?*

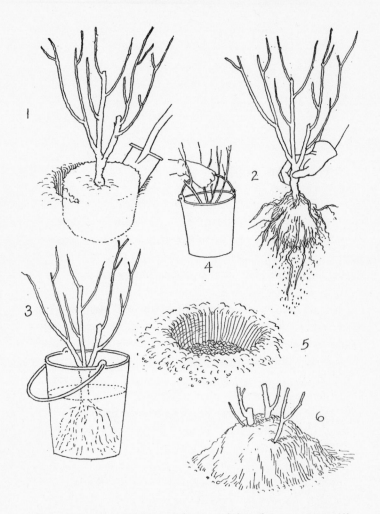

Dig a dormant rose deep enough to get below the root system (1), shake off soil (2), put the rose in a pail of water (3, 4) and replant it in the new location (5). Hill up as you would a new rose (6).

A. Yes, but only if you handle them properly. If you wish to move a rosebush during its growing season, keep in mind that you will be setting it back probably for the remainder of the season. However, if the job must be done, it can be done without permanent injury.

Q. *How should a plant be moved during the growing season?*

A. First, prepare the hole at the new location. Then, dig all around the plant, levering gently with a spade or shovel to loosen the plant from the soil. Lift the plant on the shovel, not with your hands on the canes, and take as much soil with the plant as you can. Carry it to the new spot and set into the hole. Fill in around it and firm the soil with your hands. Finally, cut away all the canes just as you would in spring, leaving about 12 inches of each cane on the plant, and mound soil into the canes. Some people prefer to cut the canes back before moving the plant from its first location, thus making the rest of the job a bit easier. A rose plant moved during the growing season receives quite a shock and needs time to recover. Cutting the canes and hilling them with soil help the plant to re-establish itself.

31. MOVING OLD BUSHES

Q. *We are moving in December. Can we carry along some of our favorite old rose bushes for planting next spring at our new house?*

A. If these roses are really your favorites, be kind to them and leave them where they are! But if you insist on taking them with you, plant immediately at the new location. You can't hold them over for spring planting without unusual procedure which would be impractical. Better to buy new plants.

Q. *We are enlarging our house and must move our 10-year old rose garden. How do you move the bushes to their new location?*

A. If you want to move the old plants, follow procedures outlined above.

Q. *My mother's summer house has been sold. The only time we'll be there is in June when the plants are in full bloom. For sentimental reasons, I'd like to carry back some very old bushes for our garden. Is there any point in trying to move old bushes in summer, especially when plants are in flower?*

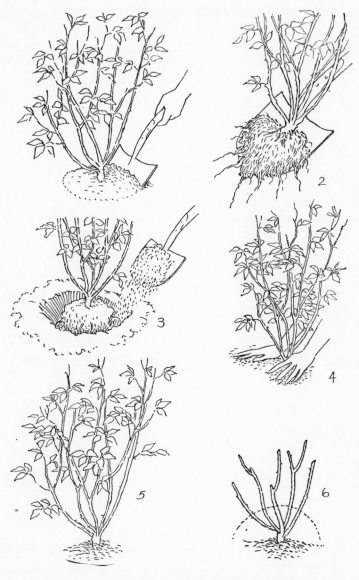

To transplant a rose during the growing season, dig a large root ball
(1), lift plant on spade (2), place in prepared hole (3), then fill in
with soil (4), firm the plant (4, 5) and cut back all the canes (6).

A. Gardens are full of transplanted old rose bushes which have outlived the experts who warned it couldn't be done. Why not try it? Follow procedure for transplanting during growing season. You'll have to cut the plant back, take as much of a soil ball as you can and wrap it firmly in wet burlap. A lot of trouble but maybe the plant will survive the shock if time and distance between are not too great. All you can lose is your effort.

32. TRANSPLANTS IN SEVERE CLIMATES

Q. *In severe climates why should fall transplanting be possible if planting new roses is not?*

A. This is not a contradiction. First, you find it desirable to move the rose to a new location (that is, it is your wish to move it for one reason or another); second, it is a plant that is established and accustomed to the climate; third, transplanting is done best when the plant is dormant, which is in late fall. Therefore, you transplant the rose rightly and successfully. On the other hand, you do not plant in fall in severe climates because you know that if you wait until spring the plant will have a whole season to grow and establish itself to meet the winter cold. Transplanting, in effect, is a necessity—planting is a choice, and the better choice is spring.

VII FEEDING AND WATERING

33. FEED HOW OFTEN

Q. *How often should an established rose be fed?*

A. Many gardeners feed their plants only twice a year but best practice is to do so 3 times. Feed in spring just after roses finish their first flush of blooming. Feed in late July or early August. Feed again after the plants have gone dormant in fall or early winter, and in any case before March 1. The late feeding gives the fertilizer a chance to penetrate deeply into the soil so that the roots have it available when they begin to grow again.

Amount of fertilizer to use on established roses varies with the season

Q. *How much food should a rose have at each feeding?*

A. Give each plant from ¼ to ⅓ cup of fertilizer at the first and second feedings. For the long hiatus during the dormant season, make it ½ cup.

Q. *What's the best kind of fertilizer to use?*

A. Roses like and do best on a well balanced food. Your garden center will have several brand-name kinds that are already formulated for roses. One prominent commercial rose grower uses fertilizer of 7-7-7 analysis for roses growing in the fields, and packages the same formula for home gardens.

34. HOW TO APPLY FERTILIZER

Q. *How should rose fertilizer be applied?*

A. Spread it around the base of the plant and then work it into the upper inch of soil with a hoe or rake or other hand tool. Water it in lightly.

35. FEEDING NEW ROSES

Q. *What about feeding roses newly planted in spring?*

A. These need less than established plants. Give them ¼ to ⅓ of a cup of fertilizer in late July or early August.

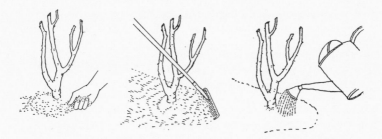

Spread fertilizer around base of plant, work it into the soil, water lightly.

Q. *What about feeding roses which have just been planted in fall?*

A. Not necessary. Feed before March 1 next spring.

36. MANURE

Q. *Is well-rotted manure a fertilizer?*

A. Yes.

Q. *Is well-rotted manure sufficient food for roses?*

A. No, it is not a balanced food such as a commercially prepared rose food is, so you will need to use the latter also. Roses do well on a 5-10-5 rose food formula, which means 5% nitrogen, 10% phosphorus and 5% potash. One of the country's leading commercial rose growers uses with great success a balanced food in 7-7-7 analysis.

Q. *How do I apply manure?*

Apply manure so that it does not touch trunk

A. Place it around the base of the plant on the ground surface to cover an area roughly as great as the spread of the branches. Do not let it come in contact with the trunk of the bush—this could cause injury.

Q. *I've been told that manure such as rotted cow manure should not come in contact with the trunk or stem of the plant. Is that correct?*

A. Yes, it is. If the manure is in contact with the plant it tends to induce the growth of fungus which might cause the plant to deteriorate or even die.

37. HOW OFTEN TO WATER

Q. *How often should roses be watered?*

A. Plenty of water will help them produce plenty of flowers. In dry weather, once a week is not too much.

38. BEST WAYS TO WATER

Q. *What is the best way to water rose bushes?*

A. Soak the soil to a depth of about 8 inches. The best way to accomplish this is to let a slow-running hose remain in the rose bed or at the edge of the individually planted spot for a half hour or so. You can get a soil soaker of one kind or another to attach to the end of your hose. These will enable you to water your plants without washing soil away. Never sprinkle your roses from the top, that is, don't soak the foliage. Of course, rainfall does this, but that is not a reason why you should. Water is needed by the roots, not by the leaves, and wetting the leaves unnecessarily simply leads to conditions which are ripe for "blackspot" disease to develop.

39. BEST TIME TO WATER

Q. *What is the best time of day for watering?*

A. I prefer the morning hours for these reasons: there is less evaporation by the sun's heat (the plants use the water

Soak the roots, not the leaves, using a good soil soaker.
Two types are shown.

to better advantage); to water in the evening keeps humidity around the plant during the night, a condition leading to mildew.

Q. *I live in Arizona where the atmosphere is dry and the sun is hot. What can be done to keep roses growing well here?*

A. In areas where humidity is low (dry climates) and there's plenty of heat, water is drawn from rose plants too quickly. This causes growth to stop, and it may be difficult to revive them. But, if you will do three things, roses can be brought along nicely: 1, when planting the rose, mix with the soil more than the usual quantity of peat moss to help retain moisture in the soil; 2, keep a thick (3-inch) mulch around the base of the plant to keep the soil cool; 3, give the plants plenty of water to overcome the high respiration rate.

VIII PRUNING

40. WHY PRUNE

Q. *Why is it necessary to prune rose bushes?*

A. First, to remove dead or diseased or damaged canes (often called wood); second, to remove canes or branches that interfere with others; third, to shape the plant (especially Floribundas) or to keep it in proportion; fourth, to prevent excessive wind-whipping in wintertime; fifth, to keep plants in bounds (as in the case of Climbing Roses whose long canes could outgrow the space available); sixth, to remove suckers or wild shoots.

41. WHEN TO PRUNE

Q. *When should roses be pruned?*

A. Prune away dead wood, broken or diseased branches at any time. A general program of pruning should be undertaken in spring, however. After exposure to winter wind and cold, there is always some "dieback" in spring. In fall when plants go dormant, it is wise to cut back

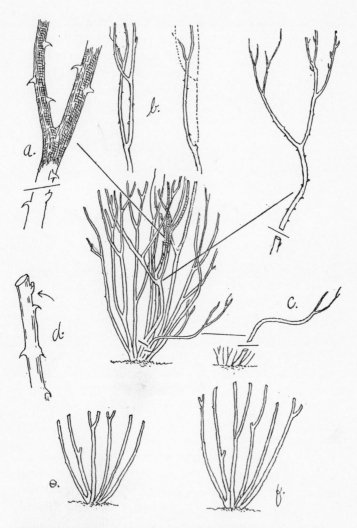

PRUNING a) Remove dead or diseased canes, b) remove crossing branches; c) remove suckers or wild shoots; d) make cut at 45° angle; e) Hybrid Teas and Grandifloras are pruned to about 12 to 15 inches; f) Floribundas are pruned to 18 to 40 inches.

branches and canes if they are especially long to prevent too much whipping by the wind. Floribundas, for instance, ought to be cut back to about 20 inches above the ground. It is not good practice to cut away too much wood in fall because there will be dieback during the winter, and in spring it will be necessary to cut back still further.

42. PRUNING ROSES PLANTED IN FALL

Q. *My roses were planted last fall. Shall I prune them this spring?*

A. In spring, always prune back to live wood; that is, remove all dead wood, and any broken branches.

43. PRUNING AND STEMS

Q. *Is there any way to prune so that I get longer stems on flowers?*

A. Pruning does not affect stems on flowers. If you want long-stemmed roses, plant varieties known to have long stems. This information is best found in the catalogue descriptions of commercial rose growers. Most Hybrid Teas do have long stems and make good cutting, but some varieties are better for this purpose than others.

Q. *I sometimes have roses growing between branches on very short stems. How can I prevent this from happening?*

A. Prune out the weak shoots.

Q. *Does pruning affect the production of rose buds?*

A. Yes—pruning reduces the production of rose buds. On the other hand, it stimulates the growth of new branches below the cut.

Q. *How can I cut long-stemmed flowers for an arrangement without harming future growth?*

A. The more stem you take, the less chance you have for more blooms from that stem or cane. Always try to leave on the cane at least 2 sets of leaves below the point of the cut. The more foliage you leave the better for the plant.

44. HOW TO PRUNE

Q. *How should roses be pruned?*

A. It is best to cut at a 45° angle because it is the most efficient cut. There is less likelihood of mashing or bruising the canes. In the case of dead wood, cut back to live wood, and make your cut as nearly as possible at a point close to and above an eye (or bud). From this point a new branch will develop. Choose an eye that is on the inner side of the cane if you can to keep the plant symmetrical. Use sharp pruning shears to avoid ragged or mashed cuts.

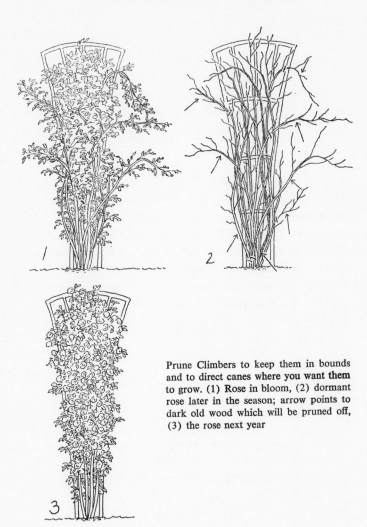

Prune Climbers to keep them in bounds and to direct canes where you want them to grow. (1) Rose in bloom, (2) dormant rose later in the season; arrow points to dark old wood which will be pruned off, (3) the rose next year

45. SEALING ENDS

Q. *Do I have to seal the ends of pruned branches?*

A. Seal the end of the larger cut canes with tree wound sealer or any other sticky substance to keep juices in and to prevent the entrance of borers. This will save many a cane. If you find a cane end with a hole down the center, cut back to a point below the hole, even to the extent of removing the entire cane. Burn the old cane to destroy the borer that is living on the pithy center. If you have established plants, it is wise in spring to remove one of the older canes entirely, provided that five or six others remain. The better flowers are produced by newer canes, and eliminating one of the older ones tends to force the plant to develop a new cane which will bear finer blooms than the one it replaces.

46. PRUNING BUSH ROSES

Q. *Are Hybrid Teas, Grandifloras and Floribundas all pruned in the same way?*

A. Essentially, yes. However, Hybrid Teas should be cut back in spring to a height of about 12 to 15 inches; and Floribundas, to a height of 18 to 20 inches. Grandifloras should be pruned as you would Hybrid Teas.

47. PRUNING CLIMBERS

Q. *What about pruning Climbers?*

A. Climbers should be pruned only to remove dead wood
and to keep the canes where you want them to go.
Climbers produce flowers on year-old wood; if you cut
that away, you remove your source of next year's blooms.
The only other reason for pruning Climbers is to eliminate
the rubbing of one branch against another, or the inter-
fering of one branch with another.

Q. *How can I recognize new wood?*

A. New wood is lighter in color than old wood, so the
distinction is easily made. New wood has a shinier texture
—a fresher look to it.

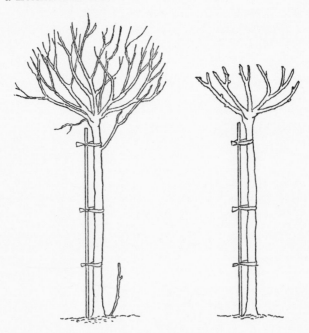

Pruning a Tree Rose

48. PRUNING TREE ROSES

Q. *How should Tree Roses be pruned?*

A. Since the beauty of a Tree Rose is in the symmetry and proportion of its head (the bushy part of the plant growing at the top of the trunk), pruning should be done to preserve those qualities. In other words, prune the head for shapeliness; and cut it back in spring to about 10 to 12 inches. Try to keep 2 or 3 strong eyes on the side branches. If suckers should appear on the trunk of the Tree Rose or from below ground, cut them off, of course.

49. HARD VS. LIGHT PRUNING

Q. *What is "hard" pruning as opposed to "light" pruning?*

A. Some expert rose gardeners are called "hard pruners." This means that they prefer to cut their plants back in spring more severely than is customary. The "light" pruning experts, on the other hand, cut back only to where they must to remove dead wood. The middle way is undoubtedly best for the average rose grower.

50. PRUNING SPENT BLOOMS

Q. *Is it good or bad to prune away the spent blooms of a rose plant?*

A. Good. Unless matured or spent blooms are cut off the cane, the energy of the plant goes into the production of seed, instead of into production of more rose blooms. Another reason for removing spent flowers is that they are unsightly on the plant, and the fallen petals on the ground must be picked up.

Q. *Can I get rose hips if I prune away dead flowers?*

A. No, if you want hips, leave the spent blooms on plant. (See section 94 for uses of hips.)

51. SUCKERS

Q. *How can I tell what a sucker, or wild growth, is in order to prune it?*

A. Easy. You can identify a sucker in two ways. Follow the cane down to its source. If it emerges from below the knuckle, it is a sucker. Sucker growth always springs from the understock, or root system, below the point of the knuckle, which is where the rose was grafted to the root system. Also—sucker growth is lighter in color and the foliage is smaller and shaped differently.

Q. *Is there any special way of removing the sucker?*

A. Most gardeners simply follow the sucker to its source and cut it off as close as possible to that point. However, when this is done, the sucker might grow again from the same spot. The safe and sure way is to pull it or tear it away from the root system, thus eliminating the eye from which it grew. Care must be used when doing this in order not to damage the root system unduly.

Q. *A gardener I know says that rose canes with 7-leaflet leaves are suckers. Is he right?*

A. No, he isn't. Rose canes can produce 3-, 5-, 7-, and even 9-leaflet leaves and not one of them will be a sucker. Stick to the 2 ways of identification given above.

Q. *One of the branches on my roses turned black. How shall I prune it?*

A. Cut it off.

52. PRUNING FOR EXHIBITION

Q. *How do I prune to get large flowers for exhibition?*

A. See section 99 (Disbudding for Exhibition).

Q. *How can I prune for exhibition without harming the rose?*

A. If you are cutting for a flower show the main object is the cut flower itself. In general, however, remember that the more foliage you leave, the better off the plant will be.

53. PRUNING FOR SANITATION

Q. *What is the point of cleaning up the rose bed or under the rose after pruning?*

A. Leaving debris on the ground under roses—bits of dead wood, leaves, etc.—encourages the development and spread of disease. Such debris becomes a haven for insects, too.

IX MULCHING AND MOUNDING SOIL

54. WHAT IS A MULCH

Q. *Please tell me exactly what a mulch is?*

A. A mulch is a layer of material, usually organic, that is used on the surface of the soil in the garden or around the base of plants as insulation against heat.

Q. *How does a mulch around roses help them?*

A. This blanket of material keeps the sun's rays from heating the soil, and prevents the loss of moisture from the soil. It helps keep soil cool and moist, so the plant's root system is given ideal conditions for growth. These soil conditions are ideal also for the growth of helpful organisms such as bacteria. A mulch, by keeping the surface of the ground from becoming baked, permits water to penetrate the soil instead of running off. If applied as it should be—a layer of at least 2 inches—a mulch also controls the growth of weeds and eliminates the need for cultivation.

Mulching

55. ORGANIC MULCH

Q. *What are the most commonly used organic mulches?*

A. Peat moss, cocoa bean hulls, buckwheat hulls, hay, straw, humus, pine needles are all used. Because they are organic, they gradually decompose and become a part of the soil, thus enriching it. Other good organic mulching materials are wood chips, saw dust and ground corn cobs.

Q. *How should a mulch be applied?*

A. Spread the mulch around the base of the plant to a depth of 2 inches or more, and extend it approximately to the spread of the branches.

Q. *When should a mulch be laid down?*

A. In mid-May, about 2 weeks before roses bloom, or at any time it is needed.

Q. *If I hill up or mound soil around base of plant, is it necessary to mulch too?*

A. Yes, but not at same time. Hilling up protects roses when newly planted and from winter injury. Remove the hilled-up soil early in the spring when the weather is reliable so it is level with garden. Then apply the mulch in mid-May for purposes as outlined in sections 10 and 19.

Q. *When do I remove the mulch?*

A. The mulch need not be removed. That's the advantage of an organic mulch. Just work it lightly into the soil around the plants in the fall before you add soil mounds for winter protection.

Q. *How often is mulching necessary?*

A. A mulch of peat moss, for example, will last a season. You will need to add mulch each spring.

56. INORGANIC MULCH

Q. *What inorganic mulches are used?*

A. Small pebbles or flat stones are often used as mulches. Although they do not decompose to enrich the soil, they do not blow away in a wind as some lightweight mulches do. Large stones are useful mulches on a hilly site.

57. MOUNDING OR HILLING UP

Q. *When planting dormant roses in spring or fall, why is it necessary to hill up the canes?*

A. When first planted, a rose remains for a time in a kind of suspended animation. Until its roots begin to take hold and to provide sustenance for the plant, the canes remain exposed to the drying effect of air and sun. It is imperative, therefore, to mound soil into the canes to protect them from drying out until growth begins.

Q. *How do I mound soil into the canes?*

A. In exceptionally cold areas, many gardeners literally bury the canes. In other areas, simply heap a mound of soil 8 to 10 inches high in and around the branches. Some gardeners form a collar of tin or heavy tar paper around the base of the plant and fill the collar with soil.

58. REMOVING MOUND OF SOIL

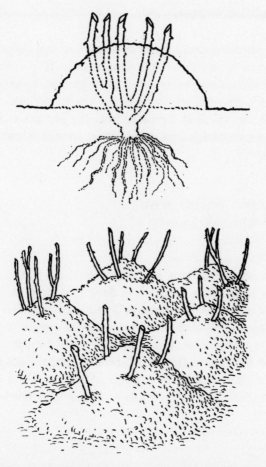

Mounding protects the plants from rapid changes of temperature and guards the canes against winter wind and ice damage. Mound a pile of loose earth over each plant to a height of about 12 inches, then firm earth. Prune the canes so that only 4 inches to 6 inches of the tips remain exposed. After the ground freezes, evergreen boughs, hay or straw may be thrown over the mounds to protect washing during the winter. Level mounds in spring when new growth starts.

Q. *When should the protective mound of soil be removed?*

A. If planted in fall, the rose should remain protected until growth starts the following spring. If planted in spring, the soil can be removed when you see, by probing into the soil mound, that growth has begun. In either case, remove the soil little by little, from the top down. Late frosts could damage new growth if the mound is removed too quickly.

59. MOUNDING POTTED ROSE

Q. *Is it necessary to mound a potted rose?*

A. No. Potted roses are sold only when they are in growth and at times of the year when danger of frosts is slight or non-existent. There could be a rare exception, however (although there ought not be), when a potted rose is newly potted and sold before growth begins. In such cases, mound the canes. The theory behind potted roses is to provide plants that have been started for you. There is no advantage to you in buying them if they have not begun to grow.

X SEASON BY SEASON CARE

Q. *What is the effect of weather in general—heat, cold, humidity—on the growth of roses?*

A. Weather affects roses in much the same way it affects people. Cool weather makes people active; hot, humid weather makes them sluggish. Roses grow best when nights are cool and days are sunny and not too warm. Their growing rate is determined by the rate of flow of sap through their systems, and this is determined by heat. The faster food is circulated by the flow of liquid, the greater the growth. Thus, in warm weather the respiratory process and growth are rapid; and in cool weather they are slow. When the atmosphere is humid, respiration tends to slow down. Also when the temperature of the earth around the roots of a rose approaches 65° or so, the roots cannot absorb nutrients as well as when the temperature is lower. When the weather becomes cold enough, all growth ceases and the plant goes dormant.

60. SUMMER CARE OF ROSES

Q. *What care do roses need in summer?*

A. Spray in dry weather (spray sticks better then). Dust in humid weather or when foliage is wet.

Be sure plants have lots of water since respiration is fast during hot weather.

Insulate the ground from the sun by applying a 2-inch mulch.

61. WINTER CARE OF ROSES

Q. *Is special care needed in winter?*

A. Yes, in some areas of the country.

Q. *How can I determine if protection is necessary?*

A. In those areas of the country where the temperature seldom goes below zero, winter protection is unnecessary. This is especially true if plants go into their dormant period in a healthy condition and with energy stored in their systems. Such a state would, of course, be the result of proper feeding, watering and disease and insect-protection during the growing season. In colder areas such as the New England and North Central states, roses will survive far-below-zero temperatures if adequately protected.

Q. *How should roses be given winter protection?*

A. Bury them completely if possible, after they go dormant. Some northern gardeners build a wire netting around their rose beds and fill the area with leaves. At the bottom of each plant, they place a tin can with poison in it to kill mice that are tempted to winter over in the leaves. This prevents damage to rose canes caused by gnawing of the bark by mice. These methods apply to bush roses such as Hybrid Teas, Grandifloras and Floribundas.

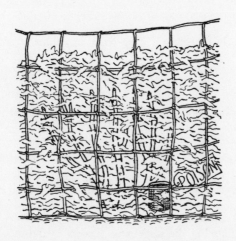

Wire netting and poison protect the roses in winter

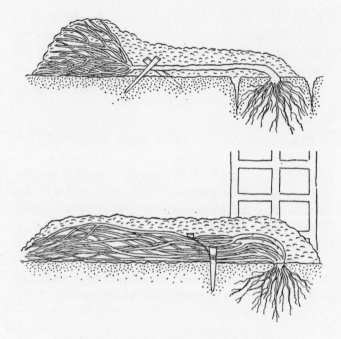

Trunk of dormant Tree Rose is pegged to ground,
and entire plant is covered with soil

Q. *How do I protect a Tree Rose in winter? Cold areas?*

A. Loosen the roots of the plant on one side after the
plant goes dormant, bend the trunk to the ground and
peg it there. Then bury the entire plant with soil or other
material.

Q. *How can I protect Climbers in winter?*

A. Same treatment as for Tree Roses above. Climbers
can be treated in the same way. Except in the most severe
climates, it is unnecessary to protect hedge roses.

62. SPRING CARE OF ROSES

Q. *What care do roses require during spring when they are growing?*

A. Once a week water when not enough rain falls. Spray or dust once a week for protection against insects and diseases, and prune in spring. Feed in April and again in July.

Q. *How often should a rose be watered during the growing season?*

A. Roses need a lot of water. Most gardeners fail to give them enough. A general guide would be: if there is little or no rainfall in a week's time, water the plant thoroughly. This means so that the soil is wet to a depth of 8 inches or so.

Q. *How can I tell if soil is wet to depth of 8 inches?*

A. A simple way would be to thrust a trowel into the soil and wedge it to 1 side to expose the soil. However, it is really sufficient to let a slow-running hose remain in the area for ½ hour.

Q. *What should I do about the mound of soil which I put around my roses in winter?*

A. As soon as you see any sign of growth, level the soil.

XI MINIATURES AND GREENHOUSE ROSES

63. CARE OF MINIATURES

Q. *Is there anything special about the culture of Miniature Roses in the garden?*

A. Although Miniatures are just as hardy as regular bush roses, their root systems are shallow and don't go deep into the soil. Therefore, give them plenty of water and mulch the soil around them. The sun's heat would affect the roots of Miniatures before it would those of the large plants. Otherwise treat Miniatures as you would any other rose.

Q. *Is pruning Miniature Roses different in some way from pruning garden bush roses?*

A. Yes, slightly. Cut them back in spring to about 4 to 6 inches above the ground. Remove any slender, twiggy growth, and of course any dead or diseased wood.

Q. *Is winter protection necessary for Miniatures?*

A. It is advisable to give them protection because their root systems are shallow. Pour a couple of quarts of sand into the tops when the plants go dormant. The sand is easily washed out in spring with a hose.

Q. *What about fertilizing Miniature Roses?*

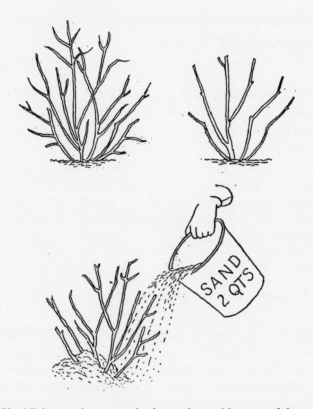

Give Miniatures winter protection by pouring sand into tops of dormant
plants. Cut canes back in the spring to about
4 to 6 inches above ground.

A. They don't need as much as the big roses. Feed them lightly several times a season.

Q. *Can a Miniature plant that's growing in the garden in summer be brought into the house and into bloom in the winter?*

A. Yes, indeed. Here's how to do it: let dormant plant remain in garden for 4 to 6 weeks. Then dig it up and pot it in well-prepared soil, using a roomy pot. Average garden soil with humus added will do. Culture is the same as described above and below.

Q. *Is there a Climbing Miniature Rose?*

A. Yes. It is like the garden Miniature in all details except that it can be trained to a trellis and will grow several feet in height. This is a fairly new development in Miniature Roses. Culture is the same as for other Miniatures.

Q. *Are Miniature roses good as patio plants growing in pots?*

A. Yes. Whether in pots or windowboxes, be sure drainage is provided and give them daily watering.

Q. *I've seen Miniature roses growing indoors. What conditions are needed?*

Keep pebbles moist and water plant from the top to keep Miniature
thriving on the window sill

A. Miniatures can be grown indoors in winter provided
that they have a sunny window; morning sun is preferred.
Room temperature should not be above 70°. Avoid a
window that has a radiator under it. The next requirement
is proper watering. The soil in the pot should be neither
soggy nor dry. Check daily, water thoroughly when needed.
An important requirement for growing Miniature Roses
indoors is humidity. This is generally difficult to manage
indoors in winter. However, it can be provided by placing
pebbles in a tray, adding water to a point just below
the tops of the pebbles, and setting the pot, or pots, on
the pebbles. The bottom of the pot should not touch the
water, all watering of the plant being done from the top.

The purpose of the high humidity is to prevent the foliage from drying out. An inch of sand, gravel or perlite is an acceptable substitute for pebbles.

64. DIFFERENCE BETWEEN GARDEN AND GREENHOUSE ROSES

Q. *Why can't I buy at a florist's cut roses like those I grow in my garden?*

A. Roses grown in the garden flourish under the high light intensities of full sunshine (as high as 12,000 foot candles on a bright day). They are by nature high-light growers. As light intensities decrease in the fall, the garden rose ceases to grow. In effect, it hibernates. The greenhouse rose, on the other hand, must be able to grow in low light intensities when garden flowers are not in bloom. Fortunately some roses can. Rose breeders look for qualities in new roses under test to decide whether they are better suited to use outdoors or in. It is rare when the same rose succeeds in the garden and in the greenhouse.

Q. *Has any rose performed well as a garden and as a greenhouse rose?*

A. The Floribunda, Fire King, is being grown successfully in both garden and greenhouse.

Q. *What other qualities, if any, are needed for greenhouse-growing of cut roses?*

A. Ability to grow under greenhouse conditions is only 1 of several requirements. The rose must have long stems; the substance and texture of its petals must be tough enough to enable the cut blooms to ship well without bruising; and (of extreme importance) the rose must be able to absorb water readily so that it will last a long time. Many roses have 1 or more, but not all, of the required qualities.

XII GROWING ROSES ORGANICALLY

Q. *After reading Rachel Carson's book I became interested in growing roses organically. How do I begin?*

A. Throw away the chemicals used to control insects: start a compost heap; use a mulch.

Q. *Can good roses be grown by organic methods?*

A. Yes. Many a gardener using no chemical fertilizers, sprays or dusts grows marvelous roses. His theory is that nature's own food and water produce plants so healthy that they can ward off insects and diseases without other protection.

Q. *How is the soil prepared for growing roses organically?*

A. Organic gardeners may work harder in advance than other gardeners, but their results are impressive. If you wish to try their method, dig the hole or the bed at least 30 inches deep. Fill the hole with a mixture of ⅔ good garden soil and ⅓ compost, leaf mold or well-rotted cow manure. Mix into this as fertilizer 1 pound of rock phosphate for each hole or for each 4 linear feet of bed. Let the prepared soil remain unplanted for from 6 to 8 weeks. Then remove enough soil so that the plant can be set in comfortably, and plant as usual.

Q. *Where can I find rock phosphate?*

A. Check farm supply stores and local nurserymen.

Q. *What other feeding is involved in the organic method?*

A. Every other year in spring, add a 2-inch layer of rotted manure or compost to the soil surface and dig it into the upper 3 or 4 inches of soil lightly. Many organic gardeners use various food mixtures that include fish meal, dried blood, cottonseed meal, bone meal and shredded seaweed.

Q. *Why does mulching play a big part in organic rose growing?*

A. A 2-inch layer of cocoa bean shells maintained year around is effective to keep moisture in the soil, to keep it cool, to prevent baking of the soil surface, and to keep weeds down. Ground corn cobs, peat moss and other organic materials are good also.

Q. *What about watering?*

A. Watering for the organic gardener is the same as for the nonorganic gardener. The possible exception is that some organic gardeners may be more dedicated than other gardeners and more keenly aware of the plant's need for water. Therefore he sees to it that his plants get all they need every week. However, the opposite may also be true—many organic gardeners rely on natural rainfall to supply needed water.

Q. *If insects attack roses is there anything an organic gardener can do?*

A. Yes, beetle traps, picking the insects off by hand and radical pruning of infested canes are all practicable for organic gardeners.

Q. *I read in a health-food magazine that rose hips are full of vitamins. How do I prune to get rose hips?*

A. Don't cut away dead flowers. They produce the hips you want. (See section 94 on using rose hips.)

Q. *I have read that some of the natural gardeners use stones or rocks as a mulch. What is the advantage of this type of mulch?*

A. Stones prevent soil erosion. They keep away heat of sun during the day but give off the stored heat during the cooler nights of early spring and autumn. They are one of the mulches which nature supplies. Many consider stone mulches are highly decorative.

XIII INSECTS, DISEASES AND REMEDIES

In *Hamlet,* Shakespeare speaks of ". . . The heartache and the thousand natural shocks that flesh is heir to . . ." (Note the word natural). Among such "shocks" endured by the human race, in its course from the "cradle to the grave," are a host of insects, diseases and even remedies. We manage to survive almost all of them . . . measles, mumps, poison ivy, mosquitos, cuts, bruises, common colds, viruses, neglect and pampering. In fact, we take them in stride, accept them and live with them.

Roses have much the same plethora of pest and pestilence. And yet, with less help than people get, roses also manage to survive "the thousand natural shocks" able to cause them malaise to one degree or another.

Nonetheless, the long list of rose enemies is a fact to be dealt with. To equalize it, fortunately, is a whole pharmacopoeia of remedies devised for effective control. The rose gardener, whether amateur or expert, need not be concerned about the multitude of *possible* sources of trouble. He should be concerned about the *probable* sources—the big 1% of troubles—the handful of common ailments that are likely to beset his plants. Forewarned against them and armed with the specific remedy, he can shield his roses and keep them healthy for years. However, he should remember that it is easier to prevent than to cure disease, easier to maintain than to restore health.

Q. *Which is better—dust or spray—to keep roses healthy?*

A. Each has its advantages. Most rose gardeners keep both at hand, and use 1 or the other depending upon the circumstance. Dusting is handier because you can keep your dust gun loaded for instant use or quick application. A dust gun does not need to be cleaned after you use it. Dust is a bit less economical to use than spray is. Spraying is, perhaps, more effective because you can get more thorough coverage with it. In dry weather especially, spray will stick while dust is less likely to do so. On the other hand, when the weather is particularly humid or when the foliage is wet, dust adheres well. Thus, both dust and spray ought to be kept on hand.

Q. *Why, specifically, should I spray or dust my roses? What is the purpose behind it? How often should I use spray or dust?*

A. The whole idea of dusting and spraying is to *prevent* diseases and to *protect* against insects. Therefore, it becomes a matter of protecting your investment in roses by anticipating the ills that can befall them and by acting in advance of their coming. In other words, you must not wait until your roses are attacked; you must prevent the attack. The way to do that is to keep to a regular program of spraying or dusting. As a rule, it is wise and worthwhile to spray or dust once a week or every 10 days.

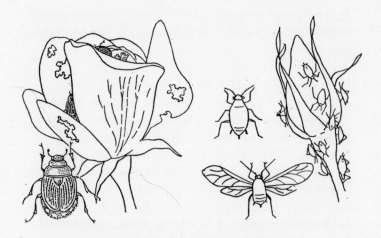

Japanese beetle and injury it causes (left); aphids
sucking juice of rose bud (right).

Try to get some dust on your roses after a rain of any
duration, especially if the foliage is not likely to dry
through wind or sun action within a few hours. Begin your
protective program in the spring as soon as growth on
the roses is 1 inch or so long, and continue until cold
weather arrives in the fall.

Q. *Since I have a very small backyard, my vegetable
garden and rose garden are practically inseparable. Can
I spray the roses without poisoning my vegetables?*

A. There is no practical method for controlling sprays
and dusts. Poisons may be carried by wind, water etc.
Read labels carefully and avoid use of those chemicals
which are potentially poisonous.

Q. *If roses are growing vigorously and producing a great
deal of foliage but few blooms, what is the trouble and
can it be corrected?*

A. This is probably due to an excess of nitrogen in the fertilizer you are using. Use a formulation with low nitrogen content.

Q. *What causes a weak neck or stem in roses?*

A. Lack of phosphorus could do this, as could too little sun. Both conditions can usually be corrected.

Q. *I've noticed that some of my roses have reddish or bronze-colored new growth tips. Is this normal?*

A. Yes. Many varieties have this growth characteristic. You'll usually find such colors in new growth in the cool weather of spring or late fall.

65. JAPANESE BEETLES

Q. *Japanese beetles cause a lot of damage to my roses every year. What can I do about them?*

A. Japanese beetles are an undoubted nuisance, but they are not as harmful as many another insects. They are not as likely to kill rose plants as to kill your enjoyment of the flowers. They winter over in the sod of your lawn, feeding on the roots of grass; then emerge in late June for more succulent fare, feeding on many kinds of plants including roses. In particular, they like the flowers, their choice being the fragrant ones. In about 8 or 9 weeks, the beetles are gone. There are various ways to minimize the damage they do. One is to attack them "where they live;" to kill them in the soil before they do damage. Chlordane and milky disease spore dust are 2 controls which, applied to the lawn, can keep beetle infestation down. Unfortunately, unless everyone in the neighborhood uses them, chances are that your efforts will go to waste. Beetles fly and the neighbor's pests will doubtless visit your property.

Regular spraying of roses will help to control Japanese beetles too. The product called "Sevin" is effective. Two other methods remain. Many gardeners handpick the beetles from the blooms each day and drop them into a jar half filled with detergent or kerosene. The other method is to use a beetle trap. This will catch hundreds of beetles which are attracted by the odor of the bait. If you use a trap, don't place it in the rose garden. Draw the insects away from the roses by placing the trap some distance from the plants. A particularly fragrant rose bloom, it has been reported by one rose gardener, actually catches more beetles than the bait that comes with the trap. Simply put one of them inside the trap.

66. APHIDS

Q. *What are aphids?*

A. Plant lice. They like to congregate along the tender stems and soft buds of roses. Aphids are sucking insects, soft-bodied and usually pink or green. Control them with lindane or malathion spray. Rotenone, pyrethrum or nicotine sulphate will also do the job.

67. BLACKSPOT

Q. *What causes black spots on rose leaves?*

A. Blackspot, a disease that causes more damage to roses than perhaps any other rose enemy. It is prevalent in

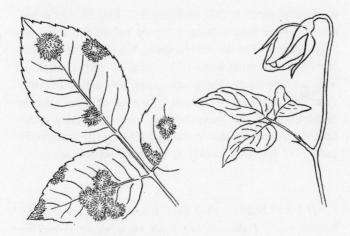

Blackspot (left); weak neck (right).

almost every state excepting Arizona, Nevada and Wyoming. Caused by a disease spore called *Diplocarpon rosae,* blackspot occurs during wet weather. If the foliage is wet for 6 hours, the spore is able to penetrate the leaves, causing black spots and generally turning the leaves yellow. The leaves fall from the plant. Every fallen leaf is one less for the plant to depend on for its food-making. Blackspot spore infection is carried to new leaves from old leaves left on the ground, or from small injuries on the canes.

Q. *How can I prevent blackspot?*

A. The fungus growth of blackspot cannot be cured but it can be prevented largely if not entirely by following a rigid program of weekly spraying. If a longish rain is predicted (more than 6 hours), spray before the rain, and again after it. The weekly program, regardless of weather, should be the main preventive. Spraying with phaltan, or with an all-purpose spray containing phaltan, is effective. A mulch will help to prevent splashing of water and the distribution of the spore by this means. Nothing seems feasible to prevent distribution of infection from cane injuries. So spraying weekly is the best preventive.

Q. *If I find blackspot on some leaves of one of my rose-bushes, shall I destroy the bush so it won't spread the disease to other plants?*

A. The disease spore is widely prevalent so destroying the plant won't destroy blackspot. Just spray. Pick off and burn diseased leaves weekly.

Q. *The leaves on my roses turned yellow late in the spring, then fell off before the summer was over. Why?*

A. A typical blackspot symptom. See above.

68. MILDEW

Q. *The stems of my roses are a powdery white, the leaves are curled and contorted. What's wrong?*

A. Mildew.

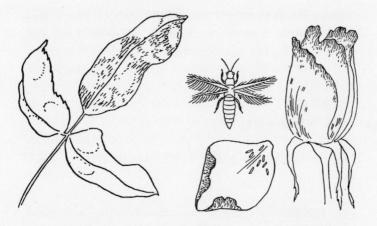

Leaf curled because of mildew infection (left); thrips (right).

Q. *Is mildew a serious threat to roses?*

A. Very much so. It flourishes when humidity is high, or where air circulation around the plant is poor. Conditions in late summer . . . warm days and cool nights . . . are generally ideal for mildew infection to appear.

Q. *How can I control mildew?*

A. The disease is characterized by a white powdery appearance of the stems and an early symptom is likely to be curled or contorted leaves. If the temperature is below 75°, control by dusting or spraying with sulphur or karathane. Don't use these when the temperature is above 75°. Better and more reliable protection is given in all weather by phaltan if the infection is light, and by actidione if it is heavy. Often a thorough flushing of the infected areas, using water from the hose, is a help. Since the fungus spore is air-borne, nothing can be done to avoid the infection. Once again, preventive spraying is the best bet.

69. RED SPIDER MITES

Q. *The leaves of my roses are discolored. What's causing it?*

A. Probably a common rose enemy called red spider mites. They're so small that they can scarcely be seen. But when rose leaves turn yellow, gray or reddish, an examination of the underside of the leaf is likely to turn up this sap-sucking mite. Sometimes mealy cobwebs are seen. Under them the red spiders are swarming. The mites develop quickly in warm, dry weather and, since they are likely to go unnoticed until actual damage is done, it is wise to use preventive spraying. Spray every 2 or 3 weeks beginning in mid-May with aramite or kelthane.

70. THRIPS

Q. *What are thrips?*

A. Like the red spider mite, these are very small insects. They are difficult to control because they infest the flower buds and often are not seen until the damage is done. Buds won't open, their petals appearing to be glued together. When a flower does open, it is deformed and discolored. A spray using lindane or DDT is the most successful.

71. BORERS

Q. *The ends of cut-off canes in my rosebed have holes running down the centers. Something seems to be eating the pith. What is it?*

A. When you see holes in cane ends and resultant "die-back" of the canes, you can be sure that insect larvae are eating their way into the canes. Generally called borers, these larvae burrow deep into the canes, ruining every-thing they leave behind. Wasps, sawflies, bees, beetles produce these killers. The remedy is often drastic: cut the canes to a point below the progress of the borer, and seal the cut ends with tree wound paint, or other sticky substance, to prevent further inroads. Burn the cut pieces of cane. You can prevent much original injury by apply-ing a sealer after every pruning cut.

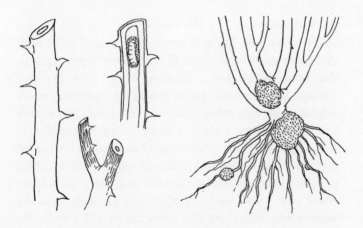

Holes in cane caused by borer (left); crown gall (right)

72. SAWFLIES

Q. *How do sawflies cause damage to roses?*

A. Sawflies deposit their eggs in small cuts made in rose leaves. The sawfly itself is not responsible for the damage that follows, but the slugs that develop from the eggs do the actual damage. They either skeletonize the leaf or eat it entirely. A program of spraying, begun early in the season, will prevent damage from slugs. An all-purpose spray containing methoxychlor, rotenone or lead arsenate, or 1 of these alone, is effective. Slugs are killed by stomach poisons, rather than by contact poisons.

73. GALLS

Q. *I pulled a dead rose bush from the ground and found a large growth just below the knuckle. What is it?*

A. You doubtless lost the rose to the bacterial disease called crown gall. The gall, or tumor, is caused by bacteria that enter the root or stem through some injury such as that done by careless cultivating or by mice or other rodents. Sometimes the gall begins at the bud union where infection can start easily. Galls are also found on the root system. An infected plant is likely to spread the disease into neighboring soil. Therefore, when a gall is discovered and the plant is removed, take out the old soil in which the plant grew and replace it with fresh new soil. Always check your plants carefully when you get them from the nursery and refuse any that show crown gall growth. By doing so, your garden is far less likely to become infected.

Q. *Is crown gall different from root gall?*

A. Yes. The latter refers to globular swellings on the roots. They are not often seen. When found they can be cut off without further damage to the roots.

74. OTHER PESTS

Q. *What is chewing small, circular bits from the edges of the leaves in my rose garden?*

A. The damage is being done by a leaf-cutter bee that cuts out the bits of leaf and uses them for nest-building. The nests are built in the stem-pith of various plants including roses. Since the bee does not eat the leaf, poison spray does not affect him. Of course, when you find a wilted stem holding the nest, you should cut it off and destroy it.

Q. *In what way is the gardener himself a rose enemy?*

A. Chiefly through carelessness or lack of regard for his plants. The gardener can inflict direct damage himself, or cause conditions that permit insects and disease to do it for him. For instance, careless use of tools will injure canes through bruises or abrasions; cultivating too deeply will cut feeder roots; moving through the roses could break branches or thorns; using sprays or dusts contrary to directions could damage foliage; too much feeding could harm the plants; bad planting methods could get plants off to a bad start; failing to hill up newly planted roses could cause "dieback." The list is long. The remedy? Paying attention to the details of good rose culture.

Q. *I am interested in gardening organically and prefer not to use sprays. Can I control rose pests and diseases without chemicals?*

A. You can try! The best natural defense against insects and disease is, of course, a healthy plant. Your best chance lies in following the rules of good rose culture and garden hygiene. Never leave old leaves and debris on the ground near rose plants, and avoid injury to the canes. Should Japanese beetles attack, pick them off by hand. See chapter XII on Growing Roses Organically.

USING ROSES IN GARDEN DESIGN

Roses are the most versatile of plants for use in land-scaping. Their special qualities are being recognized and put to use more and more as landscape architects become increasingly conscious of their value on a home property. More important than the influence of the professional, however, is that of the average gardener—the man who puts a rose where he thinks it will please him, even though to do so goes against the customary ideas of good planting. This gardener, accustomed as he has been to think that roses should be planted in rose gardens, plants a group of three Floribundas at the foot of the lamppost near the street or smack in the middle of his patch of front lawn or in the base planting itself. This is not to say that the formal rose garden tucked away at the back of the property is no longer in style. Such concentrated gardens, whether large or small, will never be anything but beautiful and desirable. They are here to stay. But so is the concept that a rose of one kind or another, according to its special attributes, will enhance the beauty of any spot in which you plant it.

Keep in mind that each kind of rose has virtues peculiar to it, and characteristics that make it right for a given spot or purpose. For instance, a Climbing Rose would be perfect for the bare garage wall, but would hardly do for the side of the front door; nor would a Miniature Rose, so perfect in a patio pot, be appropriately placed in the middle of an acre of lawn. In planting roses for best effect, it is not a matter of letting your conscience be your guide, or what your neighbor does, or what your father before you did on the old homestead. It is simply a matter of pleasing yourself and using common sense as you do it.

75.   HOW TO USE BUSH ROSES SUCCESSFULLY

Q. *Where should Hybrid Teas be planted to best show their beauty?*

A. Remembering that Hybrid Teas are noted for size and beauty of bloom, for length of stem and for upright plant habit, you would place them to best advantage where you could walk by or among them. Such a place would be in a bed two or three plants deep and as long as would be practicable either in an area by itself or alongside a walk. There is, of course, always the formal garden laid out in a pleasing design in which Hybrid Teas would be ideally situated. An individual Hybrid Tea planted amid perennials is attractive.

Q. *What's the difference between a cutting garden and any rose garden?*

A. Many gardeners prefer not to take cut blooms from their formal plantings in order to keep those plantings looking their best. Instead, they establish a "cutting garden," an inconspicuous area in which they plant roses for the sole purpose of cutting blooms from them for house decoration. In such a garden, no particular attention is paid to arrangement or to appearance. The roses are put in wherever there is a vacant spot. Roses are cut as they become available and without regard to disfigurement of the bush due to taking long stems along with the blooms. One such garden is referred to by its owner as "the nursery." Into it go plants that are lifted from the formal plantings because they are sickly or not wanted there any longer or have enough life in them to try saving. It is amazing that from this "nursery" have come some splendid blooms for bouquets and arrangements.

Q. *In planting Hybrid Teas in a bed or border, what is the best arrangement of colors? Should one mix them or not?*

A. Please yourself. If there is a rule—that's it! Some people like two or more plants of the same variety grouped together, followed by an equal number of another variety and color, and so on. Others plant for harmony or contrast in colors. Some will have nothing but red roses—or pink— or yellow. However you do it is right if you like it that way.

Q. *I'd like to create a focal point in the center of an expansive lawn, roses with a lot of color that would draw immediate attention. Which would you recommend?*

A. Floribundas by all means. These provide extraordinary color effects when planted in groups. Let us say that you plant a couple of dozen red Floribundas in a circular design, with two or three rows in concentric circles and a red Tree Rose at the center. This would make a display not to be missed by even the most casual observer. Either of the two All-America winners, Sarabande and Fire King, would serve admirably. Both are fiery orange-red in color; both have clusters of brilliant blooms over a long season. As for the Tree Rose, try either Christian Dior, also an All-America winner, or Crimson Glory.

Q. *How can I plant Floribundas for most effective color?*

A. Since Floribundas are noted for their ability to deliver masses of color, the most striking way to plant them is in groups of three or more, and all in the same color. For instance, a border of Floribundas of the same variety, or the circular planting mentioned above, or even three roses in a triangular planting, would best exhibit the beauty of this class of rose. You can mix colors, of course—but for the most impressive display plant the same kind.

Q. *What about Floribundas as hedge plants?*

A. A hedge is, after all, simply a row of plants growing together close enough to create a continuous line. Floribundas make good low-growing hedges (2½ to 3 feet or so). For more densely growing and taller hedges, use the rose varieties, Red Glory (formerly called Hybrid 311), Robin Hood or County Fair. These were developed for the purpose; whereas Floribundas, when used in hedges, are

simply adapted to that purpose by you. It all depends on what you want; but Floribundas do make good low hedges. Other ways to use hedge roses are to provide a barrier, psychological and actual, aimed at preventing cross-lawn traffic; to define a play area or a clothes-drying yard; to section off the vegetable garden from the patio; to edge paths or walks; to serve as living fences.

Q. *How would you use Grandifloras?*

A. These are so much like Hybrid Teas in their growing habit, although they are inclined to have clusters of blooms rather than blooms individually held on the stem, that they should be used like Hybrid Teas. However, since most of the few Grandifloras available so far are taller-growing than Hybrid Teas, place Grandifloras at the back of the bed. Check the catalog for the height of each variety so that you will get them in the proper place.

Q. *Is there any good reason why Hybrid Teas, Grandifloras and Floribundas should not be planted in the same bed?*

A. None at all. But avoid planting all 3 kinds in a single row not only because of the disparate heights to which they will grow, but also because "drifts" are more interesting.

Q. *I would like to plant roses at the sides of my pool. Keeping the thorns in mind, do you think it's a good idea?*

A. Why not? It would be common sense to keep them on the far end of the poolside walkway, that is, with an intervening strip of grass or paving. Rose thorns don't fall off by themselves and are not windborne. Your only concern would be to pick up all twigs and branches when you prune the roses. Plant the roses far enough from the intervening strip so that their branches will not touch people as they walk to the pool or sun themselves.

Q. *I've heard that rose beds should not be wider than 5 feet. Is this true? Why?*

A. It's good practice to keep the width of rose beds to 5 feet or less. The reason is mostly one of convenience. When wider than 5 feet, the rose bed becomes difficult to maintain, for it would be necessary to push your way among the roses to care for them. This would result in broken branches, torn clothes and scratched legs. In addition, it would be necessary to walk on soil which you should be trying to keep loose.

76. MIXED GARDENS

Q. *My garden is mainly of roses but I'd like some recommendations of good perennials that bloom at the same time and complement them in color. Any suggestions?*

A. Many perennials go well with roses. You should use those that take your fancy or that are particularly adapted to your area. An especially effective grouping can be made of roses, hemerocallis and peonies. The three garden layouts illustrated are suggested by the All-America Rose Selections. If you use these three kinds of plants you will

Three garden layouts showing roses with hemerocallis and peonies. Plant roses in groups of 3 or more (same variety or mixed), hemerocallis in groups of 3 or more (same variety most effective) and peonies singly. A group or 2 of chrysanthemums will give masses of autumn color. Do not hesitate to substitute plants more adapted to your area. *A Picture Book of Perennials* by Arno and Irene Nehrling has many suggestions.

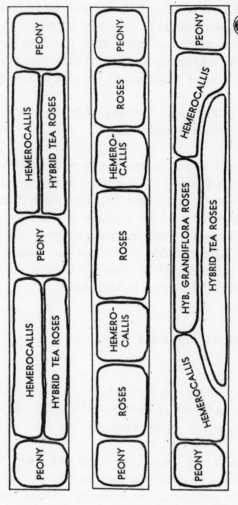

need about 6 square feet of space for each peony, 4 for each rose and 3 for each hemerocallis. Plant the roses and hemerocallis in groups and the peonies singly.

Q. *Would you name some varieties of perennials to grow with roses and give brief descriptions?*

A. Roses—Mister Lincoln, bright crimson Hybrid Tea, AARS winner 1965; Camelot, coral-pink Grandiflora, AARS winner 1965; Saratoga, white Floribunda; Granada, scarlet, nasturtium and yellow Hybrid Tea; Royal Highness, pink Hybrid Tea; Tropicana, orange-red Hybrid Tea; Christian Dior, crimson-scarlet Hybrid Tea; King's Ransom, yellow Hybrid Tea.

Hemerocallis—(figures indicate height)—Early Morn (30"), buff yellow, extra early; Painted Lady (36"), cinnamon-buff, long season; Ringlets (32"), many small golden yellow, mid-season; Golden Chimes (40"), golden yellow, mid-season; Shooting Star (38"), cream yellow, late mid-season; August Pioneer (36"), chrome yellow, very late.

Peonies—Festiva Maxima, white; Karl Rosenfield, red; Edulis Superba, pink; or any other kinds you like.

Q. *Can I mix roses with other kinds of plants, including annuals, vegetables, etc.*

Q. Yes. In the small backyard, it is hard to avoid this. Just plant your roses, annuals, perennials the proper distance apart from each other. Avoid use of toxic sprays which may come in contact with vegetables and herbs and there is no reason why you cannot be successful.

77. ROSES FOR ACCENT

Q. *What kinds of roses are best for accent?*

A. Tree Roses. Use them on each side of a path at the entrance to a garden, or at the terminal points of fairly long rows of Bush Roses. They are wonderful as specimen plants standing alone, or as the central feature to break up a large expanse of lawn.

Q. *Are other kinds of roses used as specimen plants?*

A. The Pillar Rose and some Shrub Roses also make good accents or specimens. Pillar roses are usually planted with a post or pole for support. Some kinds are strong enough to stand alone, although to look their best they need to be tied to a support. One of the better and newer Pillars is called Pillar of Fire; one of the better Shrub Roses, though not new, is called The Fairy.

78. IDEAS FOR CLIMBERS

Q. *Where would you plant Climbing Roses?*

A. Chief uses are to decorate a wall or fence, to provide color in a drab spot, to screen out unsightly views.

Q. *The gable end of my house, a red brick wall, needs dressing up. Would you recommend a Climber? What kind? How would I keep it fastened to the wall?*

A. A Climber or two would be ideal, if the wall is 20 or more feet wide. Put in at least 2, planted at least 8 feet apart. For a red brick, choose a white, light pink or yellow. Most reds or oranges would clash with the brick. Tie the strong-growing canes to a sturdy trellis. One way to do this is to build a lattice-work structure of ½ x 2-inch wood. Drill several holes into the mortar between the bricks, using a ½-inch star drill. Insert wood plugs tightly into the holes. Raise the lattice-work into position and screw it to the plugs. Another method is to buy 2 fan-shaped trellises, 1 for each plant, from a garden center or hardware store. Plastic coated metal mesh supports are also available.

Q. *I'm considering putting an arbor over a path that leads to the rear of my grounds and want to use Climbers. The arbor I have in mind has a bench on each side. Any recommendations?*

A. Yes. First, be sure to set the arbor level and solid on the ground. If you don't you'll never get another chance because the vigorous growing Climbers will hold it in its original position. It will be a case of the plants supporting the arbor instead of the other way around. Usually, such arbors are kept in position by stakes driven into the ground at each corner and nailed to the arbor. Next, keep in mind that to make those arbor seats an attractive place in which to relax on a hot summer day it will be necessary to fasten the growing canes in such a way as not to let their stems and thorns encroach upon the space needed for comfortable sitting. A Climbing Rose has a way of taking over an area. By judicious tying of canes and some pruning, you can make the spot inviting and useful.

Q. *How can I espalier a Climber against a stucco wall?*

A. Keeping in mind that to espalier a plant means to grow it flat on a support (2 dimensions instead of 3), it becomes plain that you can grow your Climber against the wall itself, or on a lattice fastened to the wall. If you use the wall, you need "masonry" nails (special nails that can be driven into mortar or stucco) to fasten the canes to; if you use lattice-work, nail it to the wall and tie the canes to the lattice at the intersections. To espalier a rose artfully, you must train the canes and branches to the right and left of center so that they balance each other in design. Training, in this instance, is no more than tying the canes in the form and direction you want them, and pruning away branches that do not balance or that otherwise interfere with your design.

Q. *How close to its support should an espaliered rose be planted?*

A. It should be as close as possible consistent with your ability to spread the roots comfortably in the planting hole.

Q. *In planting Climbers on a post-and-rail fence, what procedure in training the canes is best for the production of flowers?*

A. As the canes develop, tie them along the rails horizontally. This permits the sun to induce the growth of flowers along the length of the canes and on stems that

reach upward. Since such rails are generally 11 feet lor
a rose planted at each post, or midway between eac_
post, would soon fill the area between it and the next rose.
If not trained in this way, the rose would tend to grow upward until its weight forced the canes to drape themselves
helter-skelter. Flower production would not be as great,
the spaces between each plant would not be filled, and
each rose would grow higher than the fence. An argument
for planting between each post rather than at each post is
that the roots don't compete with the post for space.

Q. *I have a compost heap in the backyard that needs to
be hidden in some way. What about Climbers for that
purpose?*

A. Ideal. A practical way to screen a compost heap or
any other unwanted view is to string strong wire between
two or more sturdy 8-foot posts. About three strands
would be enough. Then plant Climbing Roses at 6 to 8
foot intervals.

Q. *On my street are old-fashioned, city-street, gas lampposts that have been converted to electricity. One of them
is on my property. Some of my neighbors have clematis
vines entwining their lampposts, but I would prefer a rose.
What do you think?*

A. A Climbing Rose should be perfect provided that
you devise an effective means of attaching the canes to
the post. Such a post is made of metal, of course, and
nails cannot be driven into it. You could tie wooden

splints to the post, and fasten the canes to them. The splints would soon be hidden by the foliage. Another possibility is to hold the canes in position by cord or wire attached to the cross arms of the lamppost.

79. DESIGNS WITH MINIATURES

Q. *Are roses suitable for rock gardens?*

A. Bush roses such as Hybrid Teas, Floribundas and Grandifloras are unsuitable for this use because they are too big and make other rock garden plants look lost. However, Miniature Roses, which grow no taller than 12 to 15 inches or so, are perfectly suited to rock gardens. Their size and proportions are right, their blooms are colorful and diminutive as blooms should be in a rock garden, and their blooming season is a long one. More and more gardeners are using Miniatures for this purpose.

Q. *I've seen a garden of Miniature Roses at a flower show, but never in a real outdoor garden. Is such a garden practical on one's home grounds?*

A. It surely is. A miniature garden, using Miniature Roses and keeping walks, paths, fences, steps, walls etc. in scale, is practical and fascinating for the hobby-minded person. An area about 10 feet square or even smaller is ideal. Miniature Roses may be planted around its perimeter and the enclosed space laid out as a formal rose garden or a home property may be simulated with a miniature house as the central point. Such gardens please and interest everyone. They have an enormous appeal for children, too.

Q. *In what other ways can Miniature Roses be planted?*

A. Plant them as edging plants in front of Bush Roses in beds or borders. Plant them in pots and use them to decorate the patio or terrace. Plant them indoors in winter (see section 63). Plant them in windowboxes out-of-doors.

Q. *What is a good edging plant to use with roses?*

A. Miniature Roses. See above.

Q. *Can the Miniature Tree Rose be used as a specimen in the garden?*

A. Yes, but not with plants that are taller than it is. In other words, use the Miniature Tree Rose with Miniature Garden Roses, not with Hybrid Teas, Floribundas and Grandifloras.

XV HOW TO BUY ROSES

Your success and pleasure in growing roses depend largely upon how you buy them. The home owner who buys his plants at some fantastically low price is throwing away his money and effort. More than that, he is convincing himself that roses are not worthwhile, for as his cheap roses die, so dies his desire to have roses at all. Getting off on the wrong foot like this can be avoided by anyone who keeps in mind that "you get what you pay for."

Quality roses, which are the only kind to buy, are grown for 2 years in the field, are harvested, graded, trimmed, labeled, stored, advertised, packaged, shipped—a series of operations designed to give the home gardener plants that will give him satisfaction for years. How can such rose plants be sold at a reasonable profit at the so-called bargain prices mentioned? They can't.

Always suspect a low priced rose and any source that does not seem to be a proper one for the care and sale of *living* plants. Buy from the man who grows them or from one of his nursery outlets.

Q. *What are the best sources of roses?*

116

A. The large commercial grower. He supplies plants not only to the gardener, but also to the garden center or nurseryman who resells them to the gardener. Buying from any of these plantsmen is to be preferred to any other source because he is experienced in the care and handling of rose plants. Thus, from the time the plant is dug from the field and sold to you it is kept fresh and healthy.

Q. *Is ordering from a rose grower's mail order catalog a good, safe way to buy roses?*

A. Yes. All reputable growers who sell at retail on a national scale through a catalog guarantee that their roses will grow or be replaced without charge. Catalogs offering roses for fall planting are available in August and September; for spring planting, in January and February. Growers offer their catalogs through advertisements in the national garden publications and the larger newspapers.

Q. *What are "doubtful" sources of rose plants?*

A. There are several. Although it is possible to buy from them and have success with your plants, the chances are slim. The risk is scarcely worthwhile. Just as the best way to buy plants is to order from the commercial grower or from his outlets, the worst way is to get them from outlets where plants are only an incidental item. Automobile service stations, grocery stores, hardware stores and the like do not have knowledgeable personnel or adequate facilities to handle rose plants so that the gardener can be assured of getting satisfaction. Another unhappy way to buy rose plants is to give in to the lure of low priced, run-of-the-field, unnamed varieties offered through hit-and-run advertisers.

Q. *What are "bench" roses? Are they good buys?*

A. These are roses that have been used in greenhouses for the production of cut flowers. When they are worn out in the process, they are often dumped on the market for the unsuspecting gardener. They are a bad buy in the first place because they are worn out. Worse still, because they are greenhouse plants, they are most unlikely even when young and fresh to do well in the garden. Rose plants that are suited for cut flower production in the commercial greenhouses seldom succeed in the totally different climate out-of-doors.

Q. *Are there any good guides to buying roses by varieties and by colors?*

A. Apart from your own good judgment in buying from a catalog of a reliable grower, two good lists are available. A pamphlet offered by The American Rose Society rates several hundred rose varieties according to tests of its members, including ratings by colors. The other guide is the list of All-America Rose Selections.

80. DORMANT ROSES

Q. *What is a "bare-root" rose?*

A. This common term in the rose business is simply another name for a dormant plant; that is, the dormant plant has bare roots, the soil having been removed from the roots at harvest time. "Bare-root" or dormant plants are the ones mailed to you. All roses begin as "bare-root" plants.

Q. *What does a good, healthy, dormant rose plant look like?*

A. The canes should have a lively green color, should look sturdy, be somewhat willowy and resilient and have no discolored, dark or crusty patches or areas. The root system should look substantial and be pliant to the touch. Roots should not be dry or broken, nor should they have bulbous growths. Although dormant, a plant like this should look as though it were ready to grow. If there is any brittleness of cane or root or a feeling of lightness in weight, it is not a healthy plant, the likelihood being that it has been dehydrated.

Q. *How are roses graded?*

A. The American Association of Nurserymen has set standards of grading for roses and all members are pledged to abide by them. Standards are based on 2 years of growing in the field. There are 3 grades—No. 1, No. 1½ and No. 2.

Q. *What do the grades mean?*

A. A No. 1 rose must have 3 or more strong canes, each from 12 to 18 inches long, and a strong fibrous root system. No. 1 plants are generally sold as dormant plants, and are the best or highest grade. A No. 1½ grade rose is required to have at least 2 strong canes and a good root system. These are generally sold not as dormant plants but as potted plants. Although they do not have as many canes to start with as the No. 1, they catch up with the No. 1 by mid-season and the difference between them ceases to exist. The No. 2 grade plant has 1 strong cane and 1 or more smaller ones. Its root system is proportionate. These, if used at all, are potted.

Q. *What is a cull?*

A. Any rose that grades out below a No. 2 is called a cull. These are often sold without variety names and at "bargain" prices. Reputable growers with respect for their reputations destroy culls.

81. PRE-PLANTED ROSES

Q. *What are "pre-planted" roses?*

A. This is a fairly recent development in the packaging of rose plants. The roots are "planted" in a mixture prepared with soil, perlite and peat moss, then wrapped in burlap, and finally in a plastic film. The package is then boxed for the sales shelf or counter. When you plant this rose in your garden, you remove the plant from the carton, take off the plastic film and place the burlap-wrapped root system in the ground. The burlap soon rots and disintegrates. In planting the "pre-planted" rose, you need not follow the directions for planting a dormant rose, except for hilling up.

Q. *Are all packaged roses "pre-planted?"*

A. No. Other packaged plants are simply dormant plants with their roots protectively encased in wet moss and heavy paper, the whole then placed in a box or carton. This kind of packaged plant should be planted according to directions given for dormant plants, section 29.

82. PACKAGED ROSES

Q. *Is it good or bad to buy a packaged rose that has already started to send out pinkish new stems?*

A. Definitely not good. Those pinkish new stems seem to indicate that the plant is full of life; in fact the opposite is true. It *was* full of life, but it has expended it rapidly, feeding on its stored up energy while its roots are unable to supply nutrients. When such a rose is planted, the soft new growth will die from exposure or lack of food. You have a plant whose root system is not yet established in the soil and whose stored energy has been used. The result is certain to be a weak or dead plant, probably the latter.

83. POTTED ROSES

Q. What is a potted rose?

A. Potted roses are No. 1½ grade plants that are potted in tar paper pots by the grower sometime in March and thereafter at intervals, and that are then placed out-of-doors in cold frames until growth starts with the moderating weather of spring. Protected from frosts by salt hay or other material, the potted roses begin to grow and when ready for sale are in leaf and bud. In other words, potted roses are already growing when you buy them. The No. 1 grade dormant plant can be mailed; the No. 1½ potted rose is too heavy to ship (the cost would be exorbitant) so it is sold locally only.

Q. What's the advantage of planting potted roses?

A. Because potted roses grow happily in their pots, they enable the rose seller to have rose plants on hand for customers long after the dormant rose selling season is over. Potted roses can be bought and transferred to your garden well into July, whereas the dormant plants are not available after they break dormancy in May.

Q. Which is better—a potted rose or a dormant one?

A. Neither the No. 1 dormant plant nor the No. 1½ potted plant is to be preferred over the other purely on the basis of plant quality. Both are equal in quality by mid-season and cannot be distinguished from each other. If

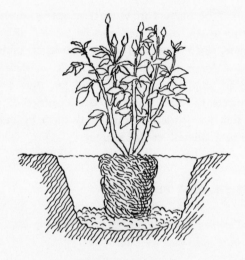

Planting a potted rose

you want to order by mail and plant in early spring, the
dormant plant is best; if you want to fill in a bare spot in
the garden when your other roses are in bloom, the potted
rose is best.

Q. *What is the difference between a potted and a pre-
planted rose?*

A. Potted roses differ from the "pre-planted" rose in these
ways: the potted rose is growing when you buy it, the
"pre-planted" rose is not; the potted rose is available late
in the season, the "pre-planted" rose, being a dormant
plant, is available not later than early May.

Q. *What's the advantage of planting dormant roses?*

A. They can be planted quite early in spring, even when the weather is still cold. They can be planted also in the fall—a time when many an expert gardener prefers to plant roses. Since they are without soil on their roots, they can be shipped nationwide, and are thus available from growers by mail order. A disadvantage of potted roses is that the gardener cannot buy them by mail and is, therefore, limited as to sources.

84.   SOURCES OF ROSE PLANTS

Q. *What are some of the largest rose growing firms in the country that sell roses by mail order?*

A. In alphabetical order, the 3 largest are:

> Armstrong Nurseries
> Ontario, California

> Star Roses
> The Conard-Pyle Co.
> West Grove, Pennsylvania

> Jackson & Perkins Co.
> Newark, New York

All 3 are old companies that have been growing and introducing roses for several generations. All issue 1 or more catalogs a year (free for the asking) that list and describe 100 or more rose varieties.

Q. *What other sources are there for mail order buying of roses?*

A. A few of the better known sources are Roy Hennessey, Scappoose, Oregon; Interstate Nurseries, Hamburg, Iowa;

R. M. Kellogg Co., Three Rivers, Michigan; Kelly Bros. Nurseries, Danville, New York; Stark Bros. Nursery, Louisiana, Missouri; Will Tillotson's Roses, Watsonville, California; The Wayside Gardens Co., Mentor, Ohio; and Melvin E. Wyant, Mentor, Ohio.

Q. *Are any of the above growers of old-fashioned roses?*

A. Hennessey, Tillotson, Wayside and Wyant either specialize in or include the old-fashioned kinds in their lists.

Q. *How would I go about finding a source of a rose that my father had in his garden many years ago, and which I would like to grow now? I have not heard of this rose since then. It is called Radio.*

A. The problem of finding a rose that is not in a current catalog is common to many a rose grower who has a desire to have again a rose he once knew. Write to the American Rose Society, 4048 Roselea Place, Columbus 14, Ohio.

XVI HYBRIDIZING AND PROPAGATING

Developing new rose plants from old ones and hybridizing or inventing new varieties can be highly interesting extensions of rose growing for the home gardener. These endeavors take time and patience, and not everyone has both. If you can find them and add scientific curiosity or a burning desire to have more rose plants without buying them, you will succeed without too much trouble.

However, don't expect to be able to fill your garden and sell the surplus to friends and relatives. The profit in multiplying roses will be in satisfaction, not in dollars and cents.

Keep in mind that you are forbidden by the United States Plant Patent Laws to reproduce plants that are patented. This does not hinder you from reproducing unpatented roses or those on which the patent has expired. If your heart is set on using a patented plant, it might be possible to get permission to do so from the owner of the patent.

There are several ways to reproduce plants, the more likely methods for the home gardener being by means of cuttings, budding and layering.

126

85. DEFINING THE TERMS

Q. *What is meant by propagating from "cuttings"?*

A. This means to induce a piece of a branch (the cutting) to grow roots.

Q. *What is meant by propagating by "budding"?*

A. Budding means to graft the eye or bud of one plant onto a separate root stock, or onto the cane of another hybridized plant.

Q. *What is meant by propagating by "layering"?*

A. Layering means to induce the formation of new roots on a branch or cane while it is still attached to the plant. (There are 3 methods of layering called *soil, air* and *tip.*)

Q. *Does it follow that the layering and cutting methods will produce their own root plants (plants on their own root systems) and that the budding method will not?*

A. Yes. In the budding method, the top and the root system of the finished plant have different inherited characteristics since two plants are involved. In rooted plants, whether by layering or cutting, the inheritance of top and roots are identical since only one plant is involved in the propagation. See glossary.

86.   PROPAGATING WITH CUTTINGS

Q. *When should cuttings be taken from the mother plant?*

A. In the spring when buds are about to open.

Q. *How should cuttings be taken?*

A. Cut a long new cane or shoot from the plant, making the cut just below the point where a leaf stem emerges from the cane. From this cutting remove the lower leaf. Then cut the cane into pieces about 5 or 6 inches long taking care to leave 3 to 5 leaves on each piece.

Q. *How is rooting accomplished?*

A. Dip the lower end of each piece of cutting into a rooting solution (your garden supply store has several rooting aids) to help induce formation of roots. The cuttings can then be rooted in several media, among them water, garden soil, sand or a mixture of sand and vermiculite. A small bowl or cup half filled with water will hold several cuttings easily.

Q. *How long does it take for roots to form?*

A. From 4 to 5 weeks.

Q. *How are cuttings handled after roots form?*

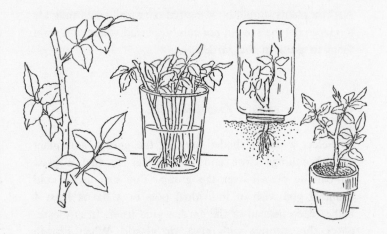

Cuttings rooted in water, then planted in small pots. The pots are
planted in the garden, protected by glass jars.

A. When roots are ½ inch or so long, plant the cuttings
in small pots using a sand and compost mixture. Bury
the pots to their rims in a protected spot in the garden
or in a cold frame.

Q. *Is any special protection needed?*

A. Yes. For several weeks afterward, the rooted plants
should be covered by individual glass jars or by a plastic
sheet. This protection should be removed when good root
balls have developed.

Q. *When can the plants be set in their permanent locations?*

A. The plants should be re-potted once and when they are too large for the second pot can be placed where you want them to grow in the garden.

Q. *How are cuttings rooted in soil?*

A. Select a partly shaded spot in the garden and plant several cuttings close enough together so that a glass jar can be placed over the group. You can use a cold frame if you wish or individual pots or a flat at least 4 inches deep instead of the garden area itself. In any case, cover the cuttings with glass or plastic. When growth begins, remove the covering. Throughout the rooting process, be sure to keep the soil from drying out. Move plants to permanent locations when good root balls have formed. During the first winter out-of-doors, protect them with soil mounds.

Q. *What is the likelihood of success in growing roses from cuttings?*

A. In any rooting process, there are bound to be losses. Some will not root; some will die on transplanting. Therefore, you should start out with more cuttings than you really want, and not plan on success with all of them. To predict a percentage of loss in propagating by cuttings is not possible because too many variables are involved, among them the rooting medium used, the care given, the condition of the cutting etc. There are no statistics to go by. It is safe to say that you will have some losses, and that as you become more skillful your losses will decrease.

87. PROPAGATING BY LAYERING

Q. *How does soil layering differ from propagating with cuttings?*

A. In soil layering, roots are induced to grow on a cane while it is still attached to the plant.

Q. *How is soil layering done?*

A. The procedure is simple. Choose a pliant cane that has just flowered (this would be in June or July). At a point about 1 foot from the tip of the cane, touch the cane to the ground and at this point dig up the soil to a depth of 6 inches or so and prepare it by mixing into it humus or peat moss. At the chosen point on the cane make a cut about halfway through the cane and 1 inch or so long.

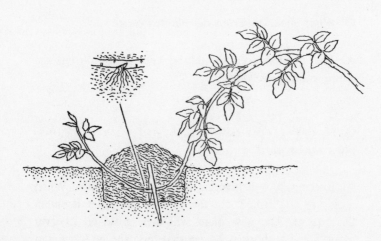

Soil Layering

To prevent the cut from closing insert a small stick in the opening. Touch the cut area to the prepared earth and plant it several inches below the surface. Then add more soil until the cane has at least 4 or 5 inches of soil over it.

Q. *Shouldn't the planted cane be held in place in some way?*

A. Yes. It must be securely pegged to the ground to keep the cane immobile. A forked stick is ideal for the purpose.

Q. *Is a rooting powder necessary when soil layering?*

A. It is not necessary, although some are convinced that it helps. If you wish to use it, simply brush the powder over the cut area.

Q. *What about watering the planted cane?*

A. The planted area should be kept moist during the entire rooting period.

Q. *How long does rooting take, and when is the new plant on its own?*

A. Rooting by soil layering takes several months. When roots are established, cut the cane at the point it enters the ground. The new plant will then grow on its own roots. Some authorities advise that the cane be left uncut

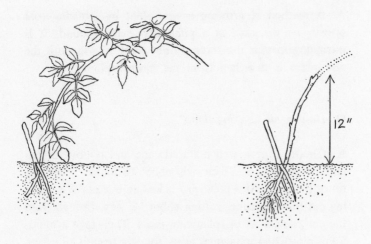

Tip layering. A forked stick holds cane in place

through the first winter. This would certainly be true if your soil layering were done late or if the climate in your area is severe in winter.

Q. *In what way is tip layering different from soil layering?*

A. The tip of the cane is cut off and the cane end is inserted in the prepared soil and held there by a forked peg. When roots are established, the cane is cut from the parent plant about a foot above the ground. This method of layering is usually used in propagating Climbing Roses, the cane selected being a first-year cane that is fully matured late in the season. The new plant can be moved to a new location the following spring.

Q. *Air layering sounds intriguing. What is it?*

A. A method of growing a new plant by inducing root growth on the cane at a point above the ground. It is intriguing in that the roots do not grow in soil until the new plant is detached from the mother plant.

Q. *How is air layering done?*

A. Choose a new, well matured cane and remove thorns and leaves along a 6-inch strip about 18 inches below the tip of the cane. At a point just below an eye make a slanting cut into the cane, cutting about ½ way through. Into the cut press a bit of sphagnum moss. Then take a handful of moistened sphagnum moss, squeeze from it all excess water, and build around the cut area of the cane a mass about 3 inches in diameter and 4 inches in length. Wrap the mass firmly with a special plastic film which you can get at your garden supply store and tie the upper and lower ends firmly enough to prevent entrance of rain. Roots will form within the plastic-encased sphagnum moss.

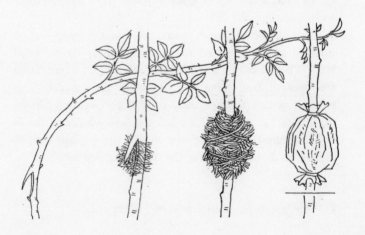

Q. *When and how should the newly rooted cane be detached and planted?*

A. When you can see roots through the plastic covering and by grasping the ball of moss can feel that the root system is substantial and firm, cut the cane just below the moss-ball. Plant the moss-ball in a pot using a peat moss and soil mixture. Remove the plastic but do not disturb the sphagnum moss. Spray the foliage on the cane occasionally with misted water to discourage wilting. In a couple of weeks, the new plant can be placed in its permanent position.

88. PROPAGATING BY BUDDING

Q. *Simply stated, what is the process of growing new roses by budding?*

A. It is the act of taking an eye or bud from 1 plant and grafting it or implanting it onto the rootstock of another plant, thus developing a plant of the same variety as that from which the eye was taken.

Q. *What is a good understock or rootstock to use in budding new plants?*

A. Many of the world's largest commercial growers use the Hedge Rose *Rosa multiflora japonica* as understocks for budding. This is a strong-growing, vigorous variety.

Q. *Where can understocks be obtained?*

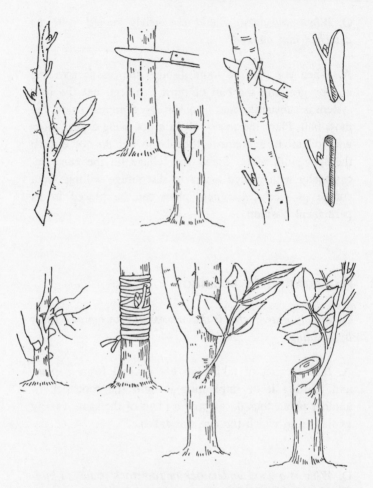

Budding method. Top row: Buds on stem; making incision; cutting off buds; removing wood. Bottom row: Inserting bud in stock; tying with raffia; new growth; stock plant cut above new growth.

A. You can grow your own or buy them. Buying is preferable because it will save a year. You can get them from one of the large, commercial rose growers very cheaply. If you want to grow your own, it is a simple job to root cuttings of this plant taken from any hedge. If you buy plants, however, the budding can be done in the same season, and without waiting for the cuttings to grow large enough to use.

Q. *When is budding best done?*

A. In July or August. Your understocks will be ready to receive the grafted buds at that time.

Q. *What is budwood? And how are the buds prepared for grafting?*

A. Budwood is the length of rose cane that you will cut from a plant and from which you will cut buds or eyes for transplanting to the understock. Cut several lengths of 12 inches or so from young canes that have just finished flowering. Cut off the leaves ½ inch from the cane leaving a bit of stem to serve as a handle. Remove the thorns from the budstick. Wrap the budsticks in wet newspaper or burlap to keep them fresh while you prepare the understock for budding.

Q. *How do you prepare the understock to receive the bud?*

A. Remove all dirt from the shaft of the understock near the ground. Wipe the shaft with a wet cloth.

Q. *How is the cut made and where is the bud inserted?*

A. With a sharp knife, preferably a professional budding knife, make a T-shaped cut on the shaft of the under-stock as low down as possible. Make the horizontal cut first, and then draw the knife upward toward the horizontal cut. The upward cut should be about 1 inch long. These cuts should be delicately made, cutting through the bark but not into the wood beneath. Next, peel back the 2 corners where the upward cut joins the horizontal cut. This is where you will insert the bud.

Q. *How is the bud taken from the budstick and inserted in the understock?*

A. Take a budstick from its protective covering and slice a piece of wood from it beginning ½ inch below the bud and ending ½ inch above it. The bud is located at the base of the little leaf-stem that was left as a handle. With care, peel away from the inside of the sliver any remaining wood that covers the inside of the bud. Using the handle, fit the bud into the T-slit on the understock so that the bud is at the juncture of the horizontal and upward cuts.

Q. *Does the bud need to be fastened in position?*

A. Yes. Take a rubber band, a piece of moistened raffia or loosely woven string and tie the bud in place, making sure that the edges of the T-cut hold securely the sliver that carries the bud. Tie above and below the bud but do not cover the bud.

Q. *How do you tell if the bud has "taken"?*

A. Inspect the budding in about 10 days or 2 weeks. If the stem handle has turned yellow or fallen off and the bud itself appears to be still green, the bud has "taken." If the bud is black or darkly discolored, it has died, and you will have to try again. In this instance, you can use the same understock again, making your T-cut on the opposite side of the shaft and proceeding as before.

Q. *Should the fastening be removed from the inserted bud? When?*

A. Several weeks after you are certain that the bud union has been successful, remove the raffia or string. Unless you do, there is danger that the understock will be girdled as it grows and the tie tightens. If the tie is made with a rubber band, there is no danger.

Q. *When should the top growth of the understock be removed from the plant?*

A. Leave the top growth on the understock until the following spring. Remove when danger of frost has passed. Your new plant is then on its own.

89. ROSE GROWING FROM SEED

Q. *Is rose growing from seed practical for the home gardener?*

A. Not really. In the first place, there is no real point in it because the seeds of Hybrid Roses do not produce plants that are true to or like the parent plant. Secondly, the time and effort involved weighed against the random result would seem to be out of proportion. It is far more interesting to try your hand at hybridizing with a purpose —the creation of a new rose variety.

90. HYBRIDIZING

Q. *What procedure is followed in creating a new rose variety?*

A. The pollen of 1 variety is placed upon the stigma of another. Fertilization occurs and seed is produced. When planted, this seed develops into a new variety. If you then wished to grow many plants of the same variety, you would take buds from your new plant, and using understocks follow the budding procedure described above.

Q. *Is it true that both the male and female reproductive organs are present in the same plant and that, therefore, it is possible to use a given rose as either the male or female parent?*

A. Yes. Each rose flower has stamens (the male organ that bears the pollen) and stigmas (the female organ that receives the pollen). The plant from which you take the pollen is the male parent; the plant on whose stigmas you place the pollen is the female.

Q. *How does fertilization occur?*

A. When a grain of pollen touches the stigma, a microscopic hollow filament or tube grows down inside the style. When it reaches the egg cell, the sperm cell inside the tube fertilizes the egg and an embryo begins to develop. This becomes the seed. You obtain the seed from the ripened hip or seed pod.

Q. *What are the mechanics of applying the pollen to the stigma?*

A. You can improvise if you like, but the procedure followed by professionals is to use scissors to remove the petals, tweezers to remove the ring of stamens from around the stigma and a small, soft, sable paintbrush to transfer the pollen. Another necessity is some small waxed paper bags. These are used to protect the stigma of the rose from accidental pollination during the time between removal of the stamens and the intended pollination. This time interval is usually 1 day or 2. When the stigma is sticky, the time is right for pollination. Remove the paper bag, apply the pollen and put the bag over the stigma again, where it should remain for 1 week or so.

Q. *How does one collect the pollen?*

A. From the male parent plant that you have chosen, remove the petals of a bloom as it is about to begin opening. Using the tweezers, pluck the stamens from the shorn flower head and place them in a small envelope (it could be 1 of the waxed paper bags). As the stamens dry, the pollen will fall off. It is then ready for use.

Q. *What's the best method for keeping track of the crosses one is making?*

A. Tie a small tag on each plant after the cross is made. Write on it the names of both parents, and a serial number. Then, in a notebook list the numbers in consecutive order and record after each the details of the cross: the date, the names of both parents, any special purpose you had in mind in cross-breeding those varieties.

Q. *Assuming that a seed pod develops and the seed is taken from it, what is the accepted way to handle the seeds?*

A. They can be planted at once in flats, or can be aided toward germination by storing them in the refrigerator for several months in jars containing moist peat moss. If you have many seeds, the former way is probably better. If your seeds are fewer and your patience great, the latter method will be better because it will produce a greater percentage of germinated seed. In either case, the planted seed will produce small seedlings which should be put in 3-inch pots when they have developed their second set of leaves. All during the germinating and rooting period, care should be taken to keep the soil moist.

XVII ALL-AMERICA SELECTIONS, PATENTED ROSES AND THE AMERICAN ROSE SOCIETY

All-America award winners and patented roses are deeply significant to gardeners. All-America winners, for instance, are reliable choices for any gardener no matter where he lives. They have proved themselves in competition in widely scattered parts of the country. On the other hand, the importance of the patented rose lies not in that it is patented, but in the reason for patenting it. Both the All-America competition and the Plant Patent Act make it possible for rose growers not only *to choose good roses,* but also *to have good roses* to choose from. The American Rose Society also serves in many ways to further the cause and pleasure of rose growing by both amateur and professional.

91. THE ALL-AMERICA ROSE SELECTIONS

Q. *I've seen the symbol, "AARS", in rose catalogs, on rose plant labels and in gardening publications. What does it mean?*

A. All-America Rose Selections.

Q. *What is the AARS?*

A. The AARS is an organization of 26 rose growers comprising the leading commercial rose firms in the country. Its purpose is to select each year through competitive testing the rose (or roses) that it considers to be the best.

Q. *How does the AARS function?*

A. There are 25 AARS test gardens and 10 demonstration gardens located in as many different parts of the country. Anyone who wishes to enter 1 or more new roses in the competition (he need not be a member of the AARS to do so) must send 4 plants of each entry to each of the test and demonstration gardens where the roses are grown, observed and scored over a period of 2 years. During this period, the roses are scored at regular intervals by judges who are regarded as being among the most eminent rosarians in the United States. After the final scoring, the AARS members meet to evaluate the scores and to name the winner. Since testing and evaluating take two years, and growing the rose for market takes 2 more, determining the winner and making it available in quantity covers a 4-year period—a longish procedure, but both a sound and a wise one. The winners for 1965, Mister Lincoln and Camelot, for instance, were entered in the competition in 1961. They became available to gardeners in fall, 1964.

Q. *Is the All-America award really indicative of the merit of the rose that wins it?*

A. Without question, yes. In the first place, the rules of the competition are strict and are rigidly adhered to. Next, the judges are competent, impartial and work independently of each other. Finally, the competition is open to everyone. Since the plants under test are grown in different climates and soils, it is obvious that the rose emerging as the winner is a national champion, not a regional or local one.

Q. *What are the qualities on which AARS roses are scored?*

A. There are 13: Habit of Growth, Vigor, Disease Resistance, Foliage, Cluster and Stem, Floriferousness (quantity of flowers), Bud Form, Flower Form, Substance, Color Opening, Color Finishing, Fragrance and Novelty Points (qualities that make the rose different or novel).

Q. *Is the list of past winners a fair guide to go by in choosing roses?*

A. Yes—because an AARS winner even though it be an older rose is just as good today as it was when it won the award. It was, after all, the best rose among many tested that year.

Q. *How many roses have won the AARS award?*

A. From 1940 when the first winner was announced to 1965 there have been 65 winners.

Q. *What are the most sought after awards for roses other than the AARS?*

A. The Gold and Silver Certificates awarded by the City of Portland (Oregon) and the Gold and Silver Medals awarded by the American Rose Society. In Europe, there are various important rose competitions in which American roses are entered. Perhaps the most prominent award is given at the International Rose Trials, Bagatelle Gardens in Paris, to "The Most Beautiful Rose of France." Gold and Silver Medals are awarded at Rome, Italy; Geneva, Switzerland; Madrid, Spain; and other cities. In England, the Gold Medal of The National Rose Society is the top award.

92. PATENTED ROSES

Q. *As it concerns gardeners who grow roses, what is the significance of the U.S. Plant Patent Act?*

A. Without the protection afforded by the U.S. Plant Patent Act, no rose hybridizer would spend his time, energy and money inventing new varieties. Thus, the rose gardener would have no new roses to choose from. None of the All-America winners, for example, would have been available, since all were originated after the institution of the act in 1930. Before then, anyone who invented a new rose did so at his own risk because the new rose could be produced and sold without payment to the hybridizer. The Plant Patent Act gives the hybridizer absolute control over his new plant for a 17-year period, just as other Patent Laws protect the inventor of a machine. To create a new rose, as to create a new machine, takes years of work and thousands of dollars. The Act permits the hybridizer to earn royalties from other rose growers who produce the rose for sale to the public, so roses are available today that are vast improvements over those of the past. Although the hybridizer benefits, it is the gardener who benefits most. What would the average rose garden look like without a rose in it created since 1930?

Q. *What was the first patented rose?*

A. The Climbing Rose New Dawn (significantly named) was the first patented rose. To date, more than 2,300 plants have been patented in the United States, including trees and other plants as well as roses.

Q. *What are the basic requirements for a rose to be eligible for patent?*

A. The rose must be different in some way from any other rose—not necessarily better than any other of its kind. It must not have been patented in any other country, and it must not have been described in a printed publication. It must "come true" when it is reproduced vegetatively.

Q. *If I should find a sport in my rose garden that I thought was worth patenting would it be possible for me to get a patent on it?*

A. Yes. However, a better procedure would be to get in touch with one of the commercial rose growers who would be better able to handle the patent. You must remember that only rarely is a sport found in this way good enough or different enough to merit attention and further action. The commercial rose grower and introducer of new roses has the experience and judgment necessary to determine the value of the sport.

93. THE AMERICAN ROSE SOCIETY

Q. *What is the American Rose Society? How does it work?*

A. The American Rose Society is the largest flower society in the country, with almost 17,000 members. A national headquarters, full-time executive and editorial staff, a monthly magazine and other solid assets for the furtherance of the rose offer many benefits to its members. Affiliated with the ARS are hundreds of local rose societies or rose clubs organized and actively operating in all parts of the country. The ARS and its affiliates are a potent force for good where the rose and its devotees are concerned, and are an indication of the enormous popularity of the rose.

Q. *I am a beginning rose grower. How would membership in the ARS benefit me?*

A. You would receive each month *The American Rose Magazine,* which contains many useful articles on rose growing in backyard gardens. It offers regional information for the area in which you live. It details the experiences of others like yourself, and these can help you to grow better roses and to enjoy them more. In addition, you would receive once each year the 250-page *American Rose Annual.* This book contains, in addition to articles written by experts in many matters ranging from soils to rose breeding to exhibiting prize blooms, what is called The Proof of the Pudding. This is a detailed report from hundreds of amateur rose gardeners of how rose varieties fared in their areas. In effect, the Proof of the Pudding helps you rate roses and judge their quality for your specific needs. These and other publications of the ARS not only give you practical help but also keep you informed of what is going on in the world of roses.

Q. *What would be the benefits of joining a local rose society?*

A. Chiefly, there would be the fellowship of others in your area who have the same pleasure as you do in the growing of roses. At typical meetings, there are interesting lectures by outside experts, the showing of color slides of roses and rose gardens, and panel discussions on any of a host of fascinating subjects—all designed to be both helpful, informative, even entertaining. Also, most local societies put on 1 or more Rose Shows during the year, and these present an opportunity for you to grow and show your own blooms in friendly competition.

Q. *Is it necessary to be anything more than the rankest amateur to be eligible to join either the ARS or a local group?*

A. If there is any requirement at all it is that you have an interest in growing roses. If you had no interest, you would not enjoy being a member anyway. You need not have an elaborate rose garden to qualify. You need not have even one rose, although the likelihood is that your interest originated because you did have some. Of course, a requirement is the payment of dues. Dues are $5.50 a year for The American Rose Society, 4048 Roselea Place, Columbus 14, Ohio. Local societies usually set their dues at $3 or so a year.

Q. *Does the ARS itself put on rose shows or have national conventions?*

A. Yes to both questions. Each year, The American Rose Society holds two conventions and Rose Shows, one in June and one in September, in different cities.

Q. *In what way does the ARS aid its affiliated societies?*

A. By providing Gold, Silver and Bronze Certificates as awards at local rose shows; by establishing rules and regulations for exhibiting roses; by serving as a source of information in putting on shows and holding programs; by publishing its magazine, the Annual, and other material; by stimulating interest in roses.

Q. *Does the ARS aid commercial rose growers?*

A. Yes. It serves as the national registry for rose names. Without some central agency for registering the names of new rose varieties, there would be chaos in marketing new roses. The ARS checks names suggested by various introducers of new roses against those already in use and declines or approves the application. When a name is registered no other rose introducer may use that name.

Q. *Is there a published list of all available roses?*

A. The ARS co-operates with The McFarland Company, Harrisburg, Pennsylvania, in publishing every five years or so *Modern Roses,* a 500-page book that lists "All Roses in Commerce or of Historical or Botanical Importance." The newest volume published in spring of 1965, *Modern Roses VI,* gives brief descriptions and backgrounds of more than 7,500 roses.

XVIII ROSES IN HISTORY AND ART

It is no exaggeration to say that the rose occupies more printed pages of the world's literature than do all other flowers combined. This is a testimonial to the importance of the rose in the mind, heart and imagination of Man from prehistoric times to the present. Why the rose has appealed so over so long a span of time and events can be no more than a guess. Perhaps the reason lies in the versatility of the rose, for history records its use not only as a beautiful flower but also as an ingredient of everything from soup to love potions. Perhaps the reason is that the rose seemed to flourish everywhere, and that as it traveled from country to country its universal appeal served as a bond between peoples. Perhaps again the rose was a thread—a horticultural one—that linked the gardener of today with the poet of ancient times. Although the rose that inspired Sappho was not like the popular Hybrid Tea of today, it was nonetheless a rose, and so shares the poet's enthusiasm.

Q. *I understand, of course, that the rose of prehistoric times was a wild rose. When and how did the cultivated rose begin its spread into Western countries?*

A. The cultivated rose is thought to be a native of Persia. Alexander the Great is said to have introduced it into Europe more than 300 years before Christ. However, a modern rose culture did not begin until the ships of the East India Company brought new varieties from the Orient in the 17th century.

Q. *Is there any real evidence that roses existed in prehistoric times?*

A. Fossilized remains of roses estimated to be 35 million years old have been discovered in Oregon.

Q. *A friend of mine has a collection of stones, which she picked up along the roadside in a Western state, that look like roses. Are they fossils?*

A. No. These stones simply happen to look like roses. They are a mineral formation found in shale in a number of Western and Midwestern states. Their resemblance to the flowers of the wild rose add to the legends about roses, and tend to further the notion held by people in earlier times that the rose had mystical powers.

Q. *Why was the War of the Roses called that?*

A. In the fifteenth century, the Houses of York and of Lancaster fought a series of battles for control of the English throne. The symbol of the House of York was a white rose; and that of Lancaster, a red rose. There are roses today, incidentally, called York (white), Lancaster (red), and York and Lancaster (white and red in combination).

Q. *What is a Red Rose Rent Deed?*

A. There are a number of instances in America in which the rental of land called for the payment each year of one red rose as rent for the land. This custom stemmed from English feudal times when tenants paid a symbolic rent of one red rose. Perhaps the best known deed in this country which followed the old tradition is one made between members of the William Penn family in 1731. This is commemorated by a bronze marker erected by the Chester County Historical Society in Pennsylvania in 1947 in front of Red Rose Inn at Jennersville. The marker reads:

"In 1731, John, Thomas and Richard Penn, proprietaries, granted 5000 acres to William Penn, grandson of the founder of Pennsylvania, subject to the rental of 'one red rose on the twenty-fourth day of June yearly if the same be demanded.' In 1742, William Penn granted this tract to William Allen subject to his 'paying the red rose aforesaid yearly.' In 1748, William Allen sold 53½ acres of this tract to William Cross; again the rental terms included payment of one red rose. This marker is on the Samuel Cross property."

Curiously enough, the Samuel Cross property is now owned by one of the country's largest rose growers, The Conard-Pyle Company, which in acquiring Red Rose Inn (built in 1740) discovered the red rose payment provision in the deed. As a consequence, the Company revived the old custom and each year celebrates Red Rose

Rent Day at which time a red rose is "paid" to a direct descendant of the original William Penn.

Q. *I've heard that the Peace Rose has some connection with history. What is the story?*

A. In essence, it is this: during World War II when the German army was sweeping through France, M. Francis Meilland who had originated the rose called Madame A. Meilland was seeking some way to send budwood of that variety out of the country to prevent its seizure or destruction. He persuaded the American Consul at Lyon to take with him when he left that city a one-pound package of the budwood. This eventually reached America in the Consul's diplomatic pouch. It was several years before Mr. Meilland knew what had happened to the budwood. In the meanwhile, the budwood had reached Mr. Robert Pyle, one of America's foremost rose growers of that time, who proceeded to grow the rose. In 1945, at the meeting of the United Nations delegates in San Francisco at which the Charter of the United Nations was adopted, the Peace Rose made its official debut. A Peace Rose was presented to each delegate. Mr. Pyle had by some strange coincidence re-named Madame A. Meilland. He called it Peace some months before the San Francisco meeting. On the day Peace appeared at the United Nations Charter meeting, peace also reached France. It was VE Day!

Q. *In what way did historical events stimulate the growing of roses?*

A. Two events in Europe had enormous impact on rose growing by the common people. One of these occurred at the end of the War of the Roses when the two warring factions were united through marriage. At this time, the rose was chosen as the royal emblem of England, thus giving impetus to rose growing by all and sundry. The second event was the interest shown by Empress Josephine at the beginning of the nineteenth century. She sent messengers all over Europe with instructions to bring back every known variety of rose. These were planted at the famed rose gardens at the Palace of Malmaison. The result was a surging national interest in rose growing. In 1829, the catalog of a French rose grower listed 2,000 varieties, and a few years later the number reached 5,000.

Q. *What about earlier times? What was the influence of the Greeks and Romans on rose growing?*

A. The Romans had an enormous influence on the spread of rose growing. As was their way, when they conquered country after country, including England, they brought with them roses as well as architecture, law and language. Roman writers spoke of the culture of roses. Roman Emperors used roses as decorations. The Greeks were noted admirers of roses. In fact, there are innumerable references to roses in the literature of the civilized world of that time . . . Egypt, Spain, Persia, Turkey, India. All this indicates the same widespread love of the rose then as exists throughout the world today. The rose, like music, leaps all national boundaries and is truly international in its appeal.

Q. *How has the rose affected the literature of the world?*

A. The rose appears as a theme or as a reference in the literature of all nations having a claim to any real literacy from the ancients down to the present. Mention has been made of the Greek poetess, Sappho, who wrote about roses. Before and after her time, the literature is filled with references to roses. What would English poets have done without the rose? And the song writers of the world, the balladeers! More than 5,000 song titles include the word rose, or roses. An idea of the impact of the rose upon writers (especially poets) can be had by examining Bartlett's Familiar Quotations, which is highly selective with respect to lines that are quotable. It lists 148 references to roses.

Q. *In what ways have artists and artisans pictured the rose?*

A. In still-life paintings, as heraldic emblems and in jewelry. Glassmakers, rug weavers, china manufacturers and greeting card designers have been inspired by the rose. In the Victorian era, when very elaborate Valentines were popular, the principal motif except for Cupid and his arrows was the rose.

Q. *What is the background of Miniature Roses? Where did they come from?*

A. Older types of Miniatures were brought to England on trading ships from the Orient around 1800. Grown in England for some years, they were then lost to cultivation. They reappeared in Switzerland about 100 years later.

A plant of Rosa Rouletti came into the hands of Jan de Vink, a Dutch nurseryman, in the late 1920's (see chapter XIX). It was he who developed the modern varieties, the first of which, called Tom Thumb, was brought to this country about 1930. Numerous varieties developed in America, Holland and Spain are now available.

Q. *I'd like some ideas and designs for flower arrangements to use in my home.*

A. See *A Treasury of Rose Arrangements* by Julia Clements (published by Hearthside Press, Inc., New York).

THE MEN AND WOMEN
WHO INVENT ROSES

The people who develop new roses are inventors . . .
creators of new varieties . . . but the more familiar tags
applied to them are hybridizer, hybridist or originator.
These talented people spend their time, energies and money
in the attempt to produce roses that are not only different
from any other but also better in 1 or more characteristics. The work is often frustrating and wasteful, for in
the search for the new variety as many as 10,000 new
seedlings will be grown, and from this number no more
than 2 or 3 will be thought worthy of further development. It is in the process of selection that the skill of the
inventor shows itself. There are today scarcely more than
a dozen or so outstanding rose inventors in the world and
on them millions upon millions of rose growers depend for
new and improved roses.

Q. *Who are the most prominent rose inventors of the
United States?*

A. According to his record in developing All-America
Award winners, the leading rose inventor or hybridizer is
Herbert C. Swim of Chino, California. Other outstanding

American inventors are Dr. Walter Lammerts and Robert V. Lindquist of California, Eugene Boerner of New York, and Gladys Fisher of Massachusetts.

Q. *Who are the leading rose inventors in other countries?*

A. The Meilland family of France (Francis, who died several years ago, Marie Louise, his widow, and their son, Alain); Charles Mallerin of France; Mathias Tantau of Germany; Pedro Dot of Spain; Carlos Camprubi of Spain; Wilhelm Kordes of Germany; Svend Poulsen of Denmark; Jan de Vink of Holland; and the McGredys of Ireland.

Q. *I understand that, in the rose world, the late Francis Meilland is almost legendary. Can you tell me something about his career and family?*

A. The Meillands are the nearest thing to a rose dynasty with four generations of rose breeders and growers bringing the family up to the present, and with prospects ahead that the line will continue. This is, of course, much in the tradition of European families with the son taking up the family work. The Meillands have achieved enormous success through the development of new roses, with emphasis on the Peace Rose, which is known everywhere in the world. Its American Rose Society rating of 9.6 has never been outranked since its introduction in 1945. This rose, incidentally, is known by different names in different countries. In America, it is Peace; in France, Mme. A. Meilland; in Germany, Gloria Dei; in Italy, Gioia. The circumstances of its debut in America, as told in chapter XVIII of this book, and its naming and appearance on VE Day seized the romantic imaginations of rose growers. This coupled with its exceptional beauty and quality led to the high popularity it has enjoyed for nealy 20 years. Since it was a best seller year after year, the income from royalties enabled the Meillands to continue and to expand their work following World War II. A succession of splendid roses has resulted.

The family today consists of Antoine (the grandfather of the present head of the family, Alain), Marie Louise (Alain's mother) and Alain himself who is now 23 years old. Francis (Alain's father) was the builder of the family fortunes. His death at the age of 46 in 1958 ended a notable career that had been studded with deep disasters and extraordinary recoveries. Francis's work as a creator of new roses was almost ruined by an invasion of San Jose scale—then again by the German occupation of France and the closing of markets—then once more by a one-in-a-lifetime snowstorm on the sunny Riviera, where at Cap D'Antibes the family establishment is located. That storm destroyed many greenhouses in which were Francis's precious rose seedlings. Out of the wreckage, Francis rebuilt his facilities and since he had been able to save some of the seedlings had a beginning for future inventions. His death followed soon after. Among the roses he invented are such outstanding varieties as Peace, Christian Dior, Pink Peace, Suspense, White Knight, Golden Girl, Confidence, Vassar Centennial, Lady Elgin, Dr. Debat, Suzon Lotthe, Symphonie, Fire King, Sarabande and Royal Velvet.

Marie Louise Meilland worked with her husband as a creator of new varieties. Since his death, several of her roses have been introduced in America. Orange Flame and Banzai are two of them.

The future, however, belongs to youth. Alain, although

a young man, has already had more than a dozen years of experience in hybridizing roses, learning from his father. Now the head of the Meilland family and business, Alain is working full time at inventing new roses, having completed his service in the French Air Corps. Some of his creations were introduced here in 1963—the roses called Swarthmore, Crimson Duke and Traviata.

Q. *Which of the rose inventors is most responsible for the development of Miniature Roses?*

A. That would be Jan de Vink of Boskoop, Holland— a most amazing man. Now 74 years old, he only recently retired from active work at his nursery. That nursery is almost as incredible as the man himself. It consists of only one acre, and the greenhouse in which he developed a dozen or so of the world's best known Miniature Roses is no bigger than a one-car garage! Since the de Vink nursery is entirely surrounded by water, the proprietor used to close it for the night by simply pulling up a drawbridge. Land is scarce in Holland, and in all of his years of working with Miniature Roses Jan de Vink never had more than his single acre. There he invented such little beauties as Tom Thumb, Pixie, Red Imp, Bo-Peep, Cinderella, Tinker Bell, Sweet Fairy, Midget and several others.

In 1963, Jan de Vink visited America for the first time. He is a short, stocky man with pink cheeks and twinkling blue eyes. He wears a dashing, upturned mustache—somewhat of a miniature itself. His humor is appealing. In a short talk he said, "I am a small man from a small nursery in a small country. It is natural that I should be interested in small roses. The only big thing that ever happened to me is my wife! You can see that she is twice my size!"

Q. *Has any one inventor more than another been inter-ested in originating Floribunda, or Hybrid Polyantha, Roses?*

A. Yes. Svend Poulsen of Denmark is generally thought of among rose men as being the "Father of the Flori-bunda." Back in the late '30s and throughout the '40s and later, his work in the development of Floribundas resulted in the introduction in this country of a number of outstanding varieties. Irene of Denmark and Poulsen's Bedder are two of the best known kinds. Others are Poulsen's Copper, Poulsen's Pink, Poulsen's Yellow. Many others were popular in Europe. His latest introduction in the United States is Rumba, first available here in the fall of 1962.

Q. *Is any American hybridizer identified with the Flori-bunda?*

A. If having 8 Floribunda winners of the All-America award to his credit can be said to identify an inventor with a kind of rose, then Eugene S. Boerner of Newark, New York, is a Floribunda specialist. His first Floribunda winner was Fashion. This was followed by other beauties —Vogue, Ma Perkins, Jiminy Cricket, White Bouquet, Gold Cup, Ivory Fashion and Saratoga. However, Mr. Boerner is not a one-sided man, having had two other All-America winners, the Hybrid Teas Katherine T. Marshall and Diamond Jubilee, and a host of other well known rose inventions, among them Coral Dawn, New Yorker, Spartan and Golden Masterpiece.

Q. *What are the highlights of Mr. Swim's career as a rose inventor?*

A. From the point of view of the rose gardener, Herbert C. Swim's last 15 years of activity have been one continuous highlight, for it was in this period that his extraordinary success as a developer of All-America winners was achieved. No other rose inventor's record approaches that of Mr. Swim. With 15 winners, representing more than 20% of the total, it seems unlikely that Mr. Swim can be overtaken, especially since he is still actively at work in the development of new possibilities for America's highest rose award. It all began in 1948 when both Nocturne and Pinkie were the winners. In 1949, Swim's Forty-niner and Tallyho won. These were followed in 1950 by Sutter's Gold, in 1952 by Helen Traubel, in 1954 by Mojave, in 1956 by Circus, in 1960 by Garden Party, in 1961 by Duet and Pink Parfait, in 1962 by John S. Armstrong, in 1963 by Royal Highness and in 1965 by Mister Lincoln and Camelot. These were the winners—but there have been others, which although not winners have been extremely popular. Among them are Buccaneer, Montezuma, Roundelay and First Love.

Herbert C. Swim was associated with Dr. Walter Lammerts, another of the outstanding rose hybridizers of the United States and the originator of 9 All-America roses, in research and plant breeding in California. When Dr. Lammerts returned to the University of California, Swim continued the work. He originated numerous other plant varieties in addition to roses. Today, he is in partnership with Mr. O. L. Weeks in Chino, California, and is engaged in the search for new rose varieties. From these men more winners are certain to come.

Q. *The mention of Dr. Lammerts raises the question: is he not the creator of that famous old rose, Charlotte Armstrong?*

A. Yes, he is. This is one of his All-America winners (1941), a rose famed as a beauty in its own right and as a parent plant for many another fine rose. Dr. Lammerts' winners also include that fine oldtimer, Mirandy, which is known to so many millions. Chrysler Imperial, the winner in 1953, Queen Elizabeth in 1955 and Golden Showers in 1957 are other outstanding Lammerts roses. Queen Elizabeth was the first Grandiflora Rose to win the AARS award. His latest winner is another Grandiflora, Starfire (1959). Everybody will remember High Noon and Show Girl, two others in the long, impressive list of Lammerts' roses.

Q. *What other American rose inventors are notable today?*

A. Robert V. Lindquist of California and Gladys Fisher of Massachusetts (the only woman hybridist of note in this country) are well known. Mr. Lindquist has three All-America winners . . . Lilibet, a Floribunda winner in 1954, Tiffany, the beautiful Hybrid Tea that won in 1955, and Granada, the 1964 winner. Other Lindquist varieties of prominence are Angel Wings, Texan and Tom Tom.

Mrs. Fisher is known both for the high fashion of her hats and the high color of her roses. Compared with other rose inventors, she is a relative newcomer, and has not as yet had an All-America winner. Her most outstanding contributions so far are Love Song, the yellow and pink bi-color; Tapestry and Fascinating, both with bright mingled colors; and Sterling Silver, the light lavender rose. Others to her credit are Bunker Hill, Capri, Havana, Merry-Go-Round, Morning Mist and Pink Parasol. Mrs. Fisher, working in her greenhouses at Woburn, near Boston, doubtless has other new roses "on the drawing board"—one of them, perhaps, to win for her the coveted AARS award.

Q. *I understand that Pedro Dot of Spain is one of the few rose inventors, if not the only one, who has achieved successes with both Miniature Roses and Hybrid Teas. Is that so?*

A. Pedro Dot did succeed in developing outstanding varieties in both classes. There is no reason why a rose inventor cannot work in more than one class, but apparently few have done so. Pedro Dot's establishment at San Feliu de Llobregat, near Barcelona, Spain has been the source of many new roses. Best known in America are some old favorites such as Angels Mateu, Condesa de Sastago, Duquesa de Penaranda and Girona. A newer one is Linda Porter. Among Dot's Miniatures are such favorites as Baby Gold Star, Robin, Pixie Rose and Pixie Gold. Young Alain Meilland of France has developed Hybrid Teas and at least one Miniature, Scarlet Gem. More of the latter may come from him.

Q. *You mentioned another Spanish rose inventor, Carlos Camprubi. Who is he?*

A. Carlos Camprubi is rather new as a hybridist of roses for America. In Spain, however, the Camprubis are noted rose originators and growers with a long list of new introductions. Located near Barcelona, as the Dots are, at Cornella de Llobregat, the Camprubis have outgrown their nursery, land being very scarce in that area. Though it is still their headquarters, they are doing most of their rose growing 100 miles away on newly purchased acres.

The new white Hybrid Tea Rose called Sincera (or Amistad Sincera in Spain) is the first rose for American gardens from Carlos Camprubi. It was introduced here in the fall of 1963.

Q. *What new roses have been the work of Tantau in Germany?*

A. City of York, Red Favorite and Floradora are three of the better known Tantau roses in this country. They are a small part of a very long list of successful varieties developed by Mathias Tantau. Floradora won the AARS award in 1945. Many are very popular in England and in other European countries. The latest Tantau success is something of a sensation the world over, and on this rose alone the reputation of Tantau will stand for a long time. It is the Hybrid Tea, Tropicana, which won the All-America award in 1963. Known in Europe as Superstar, this rose won a dozen top awards at the principal rose trials of France, England, Italy, Spain, Germany and Switzerland. In America, it won the Gold Certificate of the City of Portland, an award second only to the AARS. Except for Crimson Glory and Charlotte Armstrong, Tropicana is the only Hybrid Tea to appear as a serious challenge to Peace, according to the ratings of the American Rose Society. Peace is rated at 9.6, Tropicana at 9.0. No rose has ever been awarded a perfect rating of 10. The rose hybridizing of Mathias Tantau is done at his nursery at Uetersen, Holstein, Germany.

Q. *What new roses have come from Wilhelm Kordes?*

A. Wilhelm Kordes, whose hybridizing is done at Sparrieshoop, Holstein, Germany, has invented several hundred roses. Without question, the best known Kordes rose in the United States is the old favorite, Crimson Glory, which is rated as one of the most fragrant of the modern Hybrid Teas. It was introduced here in 1935 and was the winner of the Gold Medal of the National Rose Society of England. Another older rose, the Floribunda Pinocchio, is also a Kordes invention. More recently, Gail Borden, Golden Rapture and Kordes' Perfecta have been introduced in America. The firm of W. Kordes Sons boasts two other rose inventors in addition to Wilhelm. Both Peter and Hermann Kordes have created several roses.

Q. *What varieties have come from Charles Mallerin, the French hybridizer?*

A. As has been the case with other European inventors, many of America's best loved older roses came from Charles Mallerin, of Isere, France. You may remember such popular kinds as Mme. Cochet-Cochet, Mrs. Pierre S. DuPont, Mme. Henri Guillot, Lowell Thomas, Editor McFarland and Blanche Mallerin. Newer kinds are Red Empress (the Climber), Spectacular (also a Climber) and Simone (the lilac-lavender Hybrid Tea). A good many other Mallerin roses have been popular abroad.

Q. *Are there any other rose originators who have introduced their inventions in America, or from whom some new kinds might be expected?*

A. Several other new rose sources are Samuel McGredy & Son of Portadown, Northern Ireland; E. B. Le Grice of North Walsham, Norfolk, England; and Paul Shamburger and Dennison Morey and Ernest Schwartz of the United States. Both McGredy and Le Grice have introduced numerous new roses in England. In the 1930s and 1940s, a few McGredy roses were introduced here, and more are likely to come from the younger McGredy, Sam. Le Grice is likely to be heard from, too. Paul Shamburger, of Tyler, Texas, has a new rose out called Pillar of Fire, and is the originator of several other climbing roses. Dr. Ernest Schwartz is a talented amateur who will undoubtedly produce something worthwhile. Dennison Morey is well on his way to a successful career with two All-America winners, Fusilier and King's Ransom, and a number of other inventions.

XX   ROSES AS FOOD AND MEDICINE

In the dim recesses of history, some admirer of the rose must have felt that the rose looked good enough to eat, so he ate it without apparent ill effect. History since then has recorded hundreds of ways, in which roses have been used as an ingredient in cookery, particularly in jams, jellies and preserves. It is well recognized that the rose hip (or fruit) is a potent source of Vitamin C, though less is known about the value, if any, of the petals. Nonetheless, the idea of roses as food or medicine has appealed to many daring cooks and self-doctors in the past, and to many gourmets and "health-food" addicts of today. Rose cookery, it would seem, is not merely a matter of gathering an armload of rose blossoms from one's garden, dumping them into a pot and stewing them up as one would a cabbage. The process is more complex and more ritualistic if one is to do justice to the ethereal qualities of the rose. Mostly, it is a matter of extracting the essences of the rose to flavor more mundane edibles, although some recipes call for the use of substantial amounts of rose petals as in jams and preserves. It is all, however, part and parcel of the amazing versatility of the rose . . . the flower that can be admired, smelled, eaten and made into soaps, soups, lotions, potions, pomade, and perfumes.

Q. *In what way have roses been used as medicine?*

A. The literature of roses records instances in which roses —the hips, leaves, rose water or other derivatives—have been used as cures for baldness, plagues, colds, hangovers, inflammations, eye troubles and others. In addition, rose essences or products were used as purges, as preventive medicines, as tonics, as love potions. How much of this was effective is not in statistical form and has not been scientifically documented. The likelihood is that if these rose remedies were effective there was something psychosomatic in the background.

94. ROSE HIPS

Q. *What part of the rose is most commonly used in cooking?*

A. Probably the rose hip, or possibly rose water which is a distillation of rose petals. It is difficult to say because there are no records on the subject. However, in any list of modern rose recipes both the hip and the rose water crop up as ingredients with great regularity.

Q. *How are rose hips used?*

A. Rose hips are the fruit of the rose plant. They occur on the rose plant only when the flower is left to mature and to drop its petals. If you cut flowers from the plant you remove the source of hips. The plant develops hips which contain seeds in an effort to reproduce itself. To

Rose hips develop only when flower is left on the plant

prepare hips wash them first, cover with water, then cook them in a covered pot until tender. Finally put them through a sieve. Use the resulting purée as the ingredient of jams, jellies, preserves, or add it to soups or other foods to enrich your food.

Q. *What is the value of rose hips as food?*

A. Rose hips are so rich in Vitamin C (in this respect they far outdo the orange) that they became a substitute for hard-to-get citrus fruits in England and Germany during the second world war. In both countries, the people on the advice of their governments gathered and used the hips to obtain the valued Vitamin C.

95. ROSE WATER

Q. *How is rose water made?*

A. Since rose water is a distillation made from rose petals simmering in water, it is necessary, if you wish to make rose water at home, to rig up a still. But this is easy if you have an aluminum kettle with a spout on it and a length of rubber tubing. First gather the rose petals from your most fragrant roses. With the kettle ½ full of water or enough to cover the petals, place the petals fairly thickly in the kettle and bring to a simmer. In the meanwhile, attach the tubing to the spout and lead the open end to a glass jar placed at a level below the kettle—a chair will do, or even the floor. Somewhere between the spout and the open end of the tubing, let the tubing pass through a container with cold water in it. As the vapor or steam develops in the kettle, it goes through the tubing carrying with it the essences of the rose petals. On reaching the cold water container the vapor condenses into liquid which then flows into the glass jar. This is rose water.

Q. *Is it possible to obtain rose hips and rose water from a store instead of having to make them?*

A. Yes. The good specialty food shops offer these items as well as many more. Among them are marmalade, jam, candied rose petals, preserves, rose wine and others.

Q. *How is rose water used?*

A. It is used in all sorts of ways, but chiefly as a flavoring for such foods as homemade ice cream, baked cookies, puddings—anything in fact which might taste good with rose flavoring.

96. ROSE SYRUP

Q. *Is there such a thing as rose syrup?*

A. Yes. It is made in much the same way as maple syrup; that is, by boiling away liquid until the remainder is a syrup. The difference is that with maple syrup the sugar is already in the sap, and with rose syrup it must be added. Take a cup of dried rose petals and a quart of water and bring them to a boil in an enamel pan. Stir in a cup of sugar and cook until a syrup is formed. Strain the liquid and bottle it. A thicker syrup can be made by using three cups of sugar to each cup of water.

XXI EXHIBITING ROSES

Probably every gardener at one time or another has felt that a particularly fine rose in his garden could win a prize. At such a moment, with interest aroused, he begins to speculate about the possibility of entering some future rose in some future show. With the vision of a blue ribbon before his eyes, he thinks of taking steps toward making the dream a reality. If the desire to exhibit did not begin this way with you, perhaps it came about at a rose show at which you saw entries that "weren't half as good" as some you had in your own garden.

There is a vast difference between the stimulation to grow roses for exhibition and the accomplishment. Most gardeners feel the urge, but not all follow it up. Other interests or not knowing how to go about it or lack of specific information or opportunity kill the desire before it becomes firmly entrenched. The budding rose exhibitor is himself disbudded, and someone else takes the prize. This would happen less often, and more gardeners would come to know the pleasure of growing for exhibition, not to say the excitement of pitting their skill in rose growing against that of all comers, if instant information were on tap at the moment the urge was felt. The following answers will perhaps serve to close the gap between the first idea you have about exhibiting and the first entry you make in the show.

97.   ADVANCE INFORMATION

Q. *What information should I have in advance of the show?*

A. You need to know the time and place of the show and the rules governing participation in it. Check with the show committee and get a copy of the rose show schedule. Only then can you decide what varieties to enter and what classifications to enter them in.

Q. *Can an exhibitor enter roses in more than one section?*

A. Yes, he can enter as many sections as he has roses that will qualify for them. Read the schedule.

Q. *Can anyone exhibit at a rose show?*

A. No one who grows roses to sell or for other commercial purposes may exhibit, unless there is a special class for this purpose. Most rose shows are for amateurs only.

Q. *Must I be a member of a rose society to exhibit?*

A. No, but most likely you must then exhibit in a class reserved for non-members. Since rose societies welcome new members and the fee is very small, why not join and compete with the best of the amateurs?

98.   GROWING FOR THE SHOW

Q. *How does one bring a rose plant along so that the bloom exhibited is at its best at the right time?*

A. The object is to have blooms that are from one-half to three-quarters open. Your observations about the growth habits of roses in your area will help you to determine the varieties you wish to groom for the show. It is a question then of how well the weather treats you and how much attention you give to your plants. Special care must be given to insect control, to watering and feeding. Extra fertilizer will speed growth—plenty of water will encourage rich growth. If you are exhibiting a Hybrid Tea be sure to disbud it to conform to the rules.

99.   DISBUDDING

Q. *What is meant by disbudding?*

A. This means to remove from the cane all buds except the one you wish to let develop and exhibit as a flower.

Q. *Why is it important to disbud?*

A. This allows the cane to send strength to the bud chosen for exhibition, instead of into the development of several flowers none of which would be good enough for exhibiting. Also, it is a rule of the show that Hybrid Teas must be grown disbudded.

Disbudding (left); grooming (right)

Q. *How and when should disbudding be done?*

A. The best time to disbud is when the bud first seems to you to be a bud; that is, when it first takes on the appearance of a bud. Slice or pinch out the buds carefully so that the scars on the cane are as small as possible.

100.   CUTTING AND CONDITIONING

Q. *How and when should blooms be cut for exhibiting?*

A. Since it is important to have perfect foliage and clean, unscarred canes as well as excellence of bloom, care should be taken that a thorn does not tear the leaves or mark the bark as you remove the cut cane from the plant.

Cut plenty of length. You can always remove what you don't need later on. Exhibition length usually calls for 18 inches of cane. Make the cut with a sharp knife or shears and avoid mashing the end. Many exhibitors cut their roses on the morning of the show; others prefer to cut the night before. It all depends upon the stage of flower development. If the bloom is ready, it can be taken from the plant and stored in a kind of suspended animation in the refrigerator until show time; if it is a bit slow, it can be brought along with a little help from you.

Q. *What's the best way to handle cut blooms before taking them to the show?*

A. You can hold cut roses for several days by tying plastic bags over their heads and keeping them in the kitchen refrigerator without having the stems in water. Several hours before the show, place the stems in warm water. Water at about 100 degrees F. is right. Remove the bags at this time and cut a bit off the stem to allow the water to be drawn up into fresh wood.

101. TRANSPORTING

Q. *How should blooms be packed and transported to the show?*

A. A good safe way is to carry them in regular florists' boxes. Wrap each bloom in waxed paper leaving the upper end open and extending several inches beyond the top of the bloom. Make a wad of moistened newspaper and lay it in the box toward the head end. Now place the wrapped blooms on the wadded newspaper so that the rose blooms are carried without touching the box or the newspaper wadding. Let the upper part of the stems rest on the wadding. You can lay several roses side by side in this way. If you wish, you can now place a similar "headrest" at the other end of the box resting it on the canes previously placed in the box; and then place a second group of blooms with their heads in the opposite direction from the first layer. Then lay waxed paper over all the roses, put the cover on and carry the box flat.

102.   DRESSING AND STAGING

Q. *How is a rose dressed and staged at the show?*

A. To dress a rose means to clean it up to look its best. A petal can be removed, for instance, if it is damaged or unsightly, and if by removing it you do not destroy the regular arrangement or symmetry of the bloom. Take care in removing such a petal that no trace of it remains at the base of the bloom to indicate that it has been removed. Tweezers help in this operation. Often there is a fleck of dust or a spot of spray that needs to be removed also. A light, soft paint brush helps here. Foliage can be rubbed lightly with a soft, dry cloth to bring up its lustre and to clean away any residue. Keep in mind in dressing the rose that perfection of foliage counts heavily in the scoring. Actual staging of the bloom (that is, placing it in position on the show table) is usually done by the show staff and rarely by the exhibitor himself. Your work is done when you have dressed the rose, tagged it for identification and

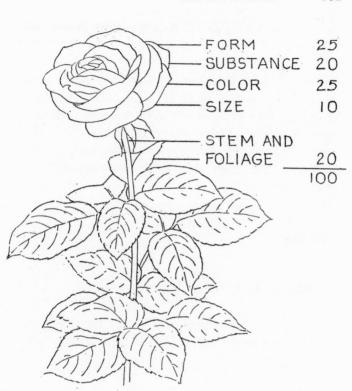

FORM   25
SUBSTANCE   20
COLOR   25
SIZE   10

STEM AND
FOLIAGE   20
                 100

placed it in a vase of water. Making out entry tags must be done, of course. In most shows, the exhibitor does not use his own containers, these being provided by the show committee.

(Since the rose is the object in view, not the container, having uniform containers places no rose at a disadvantage where eye appeal is concerned.)

Q. *How much time should be allowed for dressing and staging?*

A. As in every competitive endeavor, last minute emergencies arise. It is wise to get to the show with your blooms an hour or more before entries close, depending upon the number of roses you are exhibiting. If you allow yourself this margin of time, you are not likely to overlook some little detail which might disqualify your rose at the beginning.

103. JUDGING

Q. *What do the Judges look for in a rose?*

A. Judges try to determine how closely the variety you exhibit comes to the known ideal of that variety.

Q. *What point system is used in scoring?*

A. Points are scored as follows: Form, 25; Substance, 20; Color, 25; Stem and Foliage, 20; Size, 10. Since mere size accumulates the fewest points, it becomes obvious that perfection is the aim. If in addition to perfection, great size is present, the rose having it is surely the winner.

GLOSSARY

It is important in any attempt to understand and appreciate roses that you know the meaning of terms used to explain their principal parts and their culture. To include the full nomenclature of the plant scientist would plainly be superfluous in a book devoted, as this is, to the needs of the home gardener. The following list, therefore, omits all but the most requisite and pertinent terms. It is a simplification which the reader can enlarge upon by consulting his dictionary.

Acid soil . . . a soil with a pH value lower than 7. is acid (pH 7. is neutral). Acid soil is often called "sour soil."

Alkaline soil . . . a soil with a pH value above 7. is alkaline (or "sweet" soil).

Anther . . . the upper part of the stamen that holds the pollen.

Aphid . . . a small sucking insect, usually light pink or green in color, that congregates on the stems of roses.

Attar of roses . . . rose oil extracted from the blooms and used in the production of perfume.

Balling or balled . . . the condition when a fully developed bud fails to open.

Basal break . . . occurs when an eye or bud at the base of the plant begins to develop into a shoot or cane.

Bi-color . . . a rose with two colors, usually with one on the upper and one on the under side of the petals.

Blackspot . . . a fungus disease of roses caused by a spore that develops on the leaf after a period of wet or humid weather.

Blend . . . two or more colors in a uniform combination.

Bluing . . . some red roses tend to turn bluish as they mature.

Bract . . . small leaflike growth found on rose stems between flower and leaf.

Branch . . . the stem or shoot which emerges from a rose cane.

Break . . . when an eye or bud begins to grow it is called a "break."

Bud . . . form of growth immediately preceding the flowering stage. Also, the point where the leaf joins the stem; and, the eye that is taken from one plant and grafted to another.

Budding . . . the act of grafting a bud or eye to the rootstock.

Bud mutation . . . a natural change in the bud through which a new variety or sport is created.

Bud union . . . the point where bud and rootstock are united.

Cane . . . one of the main branches of the rose plant that usually starts near the base of the plant.

Canker . . . a fungus disease that causes areas of dead bark on the canes.

Chlorosis . . . a condition of the leaves indicated by yellowing, or loss of chlorophyll (the green coloring matter in foliage).

Cross . . . result when two plants are cross pollinated.

Cross-pollination . . . occurs when the pollen of one variety is placed on the stigma of another.

Cutting (a cutting) . . . that piece of the stem cut from a plant for use in plant propagation.

Decorative . . . term applied to a rose that is colorful in the garden but that does not have characteristics required for exhibiting in rose shows. (See Exhibiting Roses.)

Defoliation . . . occurs when foliage drops from the plant.

Dieback . . . term applied to the dying back of the cane ends.

Disbudding . . . the act of removing unwanted buds from the plant. This is usually done to make remaining buds develop into larger flowers.

Dormant . . . when a rose is in its resting or "sleeping" period as when in the garden in winter.

Exhibition . . . applied to a rose with excellent form of bud and bloom and suitable for display in exhibitions.

Eye . . . a small bud located just above where leaf joins stem; a synonym for bud.

Floriferous . . . the quality of being free-flowering.

Force or forcing . . . to encourage rapid or early growth by means of artificial stimulation, such as growing under glass in a greenhouse.

Grafting . . . the act of joining a section or piece of one plant with another growing plant.

Grub . . . the beetle in its larval stage.

Hair roots . . . very fine, hairlike, feeding roots.

Hardiness . . . characteristic of a plant that enables it to live through severe climatic conditions, especially freezing temperatures.

Heavy soil . . . densely composed soil such as clay or silt.

Hilling . . . to hill up the base of the plant by drawing soil into its canes for winter protection.

Hip . . . the seed pod or fruit of the rose plant found at the stem end after the flower has matured and fallen.

Hue . . . colors of the spectrum such as violet, blue, green, yellow, orange and red.

Humus . . . decomposed plant or animal matter.

Hybrid . . . the plant which results when two different varieties or species of plants are crossed.

Inflorescence . . . when a single stem bears a cluster of flowers.

Inorganic . . . matter whose origin is mineral, as opposed to vegetative and animal tissues.

Larva . . . life stage of an insect before maturity.

Light soil . . . porous soil composed of larger particles as in loamy or sandy soils.

Mounding . . . same as hilling.

Mulch . . . loose material such as peat moss, hay, straw, cocoa bean hulls, buckwheat hulls used around the base of a plant to keep the soil cool and moist; a protective, insulating organic material.

Multicolor . . . a rose with several colors.

Neutral soil . . . soil with a pH of 7., or neither acid nor alkaline.

Organic . . . matter whose origin is living tissue; decaying or decomposed animal and vegetative matter.

Own-root . . . a plant growing on or from its own roots; one that is not budded or grafted.

Pedicel . . . the stem between the flower and the leaf, commonly called the neck.

Petiole . . . the stem of the leaf.

Pinching . . . the act of pinching off or removing the bud or growing tip of a cane to induce branching or formation of larger flowers.

Remontant . . . the ability of a rose to repeat its blooming.

Reversion . . . a rose plant is said to have reverted when, because the grafted bud dries out, it is taken over by sucker growth from the root system.

Root knot . . . root injury caused by very small worms in the soil called ellworms or nematodes.

Rootstock . . . the understock or root system of a plant on which a rose variety is budded or grafted.

Sport . . . the result when a natural change occurs in the characteristics of a variety, as when a rose plant suddenly developes (usually on one side of the plant only) a cane with a rose of a different color. A sport is in fact a new and different rose.

Stamen . . . the anther and filament comprising the male organ of a flower.

Stem . . . the branch that holds the flower.

Stock . . . the same as understock; the root system.

Sucker . . . a wild shoot that originates from the understock below the point where the bud is grafted. A sucker will have foliage that is lighter in color and smaller than that of the grafted plant.

Understock . . . see Rootstock.

Union . . . or bud union; the point at which the bud is grafted to the understock. It is also called knuckle.

Variety . . . a named plant. The rose called Peace is a variety of Hybrid Tea Rose.

INDEX